The Heart of England

The Heart of England

Text by Robin Whiteman
Photographs by Rob Talbot

Weidenfeld and Nicolson
London

Text and photographs © Talbot–Whiteman 1992

The right of Robin Whiteman and Rob Talbot to be
identified as authors of this work has been asserted by
them in accordance with the Copyright, Designs and
Patents Act 1988.

First published in Great Britain by George Weidenfeld
and Nicolson Limited, 91 Clapham High Street,
London SW4 7TA

Designed by Nick Avery
Map by Line + Line

British Library Cataloguing-in-Publication Data
A catalogue record for this book is available from the
British Library.

ISBN 0–297–83079–1

Typeset at The Spartan Press Ltd, Lymington, Hants
Printed and bound in Italy

Endpapers: 12 High Street, Feckenham, Worcestershire
(see p. 149)
Half-title page: Anne Hathaway's Cottage, Shottery,
Warwickshire (see p. 15)
Title page: Stokesay Castle, near Craven Arms, Shropshire –
a fortified manor house built in the late thirteenth century by
Lawrence de Ludlow, a wealthy wool merchant, but named after
an earlier lord of the manor called de Say. The castle was
besieged by the Parliamentarians during the Civil War but
suffered little damage as the Royalists quickly surrendered. The
approach to the castle is through an attractive early seventeenth-
century timber-framed gatehouse.

CONTENTS

ACKNOWLEDGEMENTS

Robin Whiteman and Rob Talbot would particularly like to acknowledge the generous cooperation of English Heritage (Properties in Care – Midlands) and the National Trust (Mercia and Severn Regions) for allowing them to take photographs of their properties and sites featured in this book. They are also extremely grateful to: Roger Pringle, Director, the Shakespeare Birthplace Trust; the Marquess of Hertford, Ragley Hall; Michael Thomas, Director, Avoncroft Museum of Buildings; Ironbridge Gorge Museum Trust; Elizabeth Henslowe, Selly Manor Museum, the Bournville Village Trust; Richard Murray, Dinmore Manor; the Governing Body, Rugby School; Martin Westwood, General Manager, Warwick Castle; Mr H. P. Barnes, General Manager, Dudley Zoo & Castle; Ian N. Walden, Museum Director, The Black Country Museum; Arthur and Margaret Williams, the proprietors of the Green Man Inn, Fownhope; Captain E. H. Lee, RN, and the Governors of Lord Leycester Hospital, Warwick; Dr Peter Roberts, Warwickshire County Council; Joe Taylor, Senior Ranger, Coombe Abbey Country Park; The Heart of England Tourist Board; Shrewsbury and Atcham Borough Council; and Shropshire County Council. Special thanks go to Dr Levi Fox, Barbara Morley and Judith Dooling. Appreciation goes also to all those individuals and organizations too numerous to mention by name who nevertheless made such a valuable contribution. Deserving a special acknowledgement are Michael Dover and Colin Grant at Weidenfeld & Nicolson.

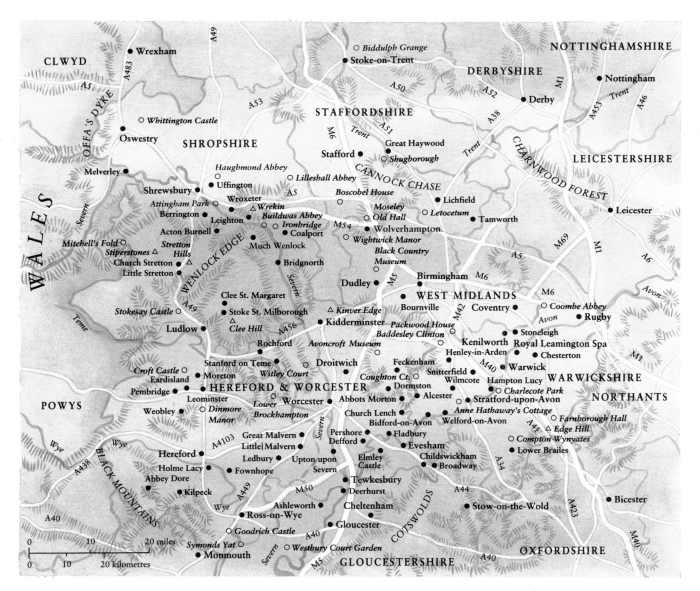

Map of the Heart of England showing the locations photographed for this book. Towns and villages are indicated by a black circle and other places of interest by an open circle (open triangle for hills) and italic lettering.

CLWYD

Wrexham

NOTTINGHAMSHIRE

○ *Biddulph Grange*
● Stoke-on-Trent

DERBYSHIRE

● Nottingham

● Derby

Whittington Castle ○

STAFFORDSHIRE

LEICESTERSHIRE

Oswestry

SHROPSHIRE

Great Haywood

Melverley

Stafford ● *Shugborough* ○

Haughmond Abbey ○

Lilleshall Abbey ○

CANNOCK CHASE

CHARNWOOD FOREST

● Leicester

Shrewsbury ● *Uffington*

Boscobel House ○

Lichfield ●

Wroxeter ●

Attingham Park △ *Wrekin*

Moseley

Letocetum ○

Berrington ● *Buildwas Abbey* ○ *Ironbridge*

Old Hall ○

● Tamworth

Leighton ● ○ Coalport

Acton Burnell ●

M54

Wolverhampton ●

Mitchell's Fold ○

Stretton Hills

Much Wenlock ●

Wightwick Manor ○

Stiperstones △

Black Country Museum

Church Stretton ●

WENLOCK EDGE

● Bridgnorth

Little Stretton ●

Dudley ●

Birmingham ● M6

Clee St. Margaret ●

WEST MIDLANDS

M6

Coventry ●

Coombe Abbey ○

Stokesay Castle ○

Stoke St. Milborough ●

△ *Kinver Edge*

Bournville ○

Avon

● Rugby

Kidderminster ●

Packwood House

Stoneleigh ●

Ludlow ●

Clee Hill

Baddesley Clinton

Kenilworth ●

Royal Leamington Spa ●

Rochford ●

Avoncroft Museum

Henley-in-Arden ●

Chesterton ○

Stanford on Teme ●

Droitwich ○

Feckenham ○

M40

Warwick ●

Croft Castle ○

Witley Court

Coughton Ct.

Snitterfield ○

Hampton Lucy ●

WARWICKSHIRE

Eardisland ●

Moreton ●

Dormston ●

Wilmcote ●

Charlecote Park ○

Pembridge ●

HEREFORD & WORCESTER

Abbots Morton ●

Alcester ●

Stratford-upon-Avon ○

NORTHANTS

POWYS

Leominster ●

Lower Brockhampton

Worcester ●

Anne Hathaway's Cottage

Farnborough Hall ○

Weobley ●

Dinmore Manor ○

Church Lench ●

Welford-on-Avon ●

△ *Edge Hill*

Bidford-on-Avon ●

Compton Wynyates ○

Great Malvern ●

Pershore ●

Fladbury ●

Hereford ●

A4103

Defford ●

Evesham ●

Lower Brailes ●

Little Malvern ●

Childswickham ●

Ledbury ●

Upton upon Severn ●

Elmley Castle

● Broadway

Holme Lacy ●

Fownhope ●

Tewkesbury ●

Abbey Dore ●

Deerhurst ●

A44

Bicester ●

Kilpeck ●

Ashleworth ●

Cheltenham ●

Stow-on-the-Wold ●

COTSWOLDS

Ross-on-Wye ●

Goodrich Castle ○

Gloucester ●

Symonds Yat ○

OXFORDSHIRE

Monmouth ●

Westbury Court Garden ○

GLOUCESTERSHIRE

WALES

OFFA'S DYKE

BLACK MOUNTAINS

0   10   20 miles

0   10   20 kilometres

7

INTRODUCTION

Town and River
Ross-on-Wye

The market town of Ross-on-Wye rises in terraces on a red sandstone cliff beside the river, 12 miles south-east of Hereford. It owes much of its development to John Kyrle, known as the Man of Ross, who was born at Dymock, Gloucestershire, in 1637. He moved to Ross in about 1660 after his father's death and, living simply, spent the rest of his life using his wealth for the benefit of the town. Among the things he helped to finance were the town's water supply, the Prospect (a public garden) and the Market Hall. He died in 1724 and would probably have been forgotten had it not been for Alexander Pope, who immortalized Kyrle's generous virtues in verse. Dominating the town is the large church of St Mary the Virgin, with a tall recessed spire, rebuilt in 1721 largely through another of Kyrle's benefactions. It was partly rebuilt in 1852, after being struck by lightning, and lowered to its present height of 205 feet in 1952. The north and south arcades date from the early thirteenth century but were raised in 1743.

Few, if any, places in Britain can rival the Heart of England in literary, historical, theatrical and romantic associations. The countryside of England's central shires is neither wild nor spectacular — except, perhaps, in remote pockets like the Stiperstones or in the west along the Welsh border — nor are the hills of very great height or the rivers fast-flowing. Yet this gentle, essentially pastoral land has witnessed more spilt blood and genuine passion than any ground in the kingdom: poets and writers have celebrated its legends and beauties; kings have coveted its extensive hunting forests; armies have clashed amidst its luxuriant green meadows; barons and petty chieftains have capitalized on its important strategic position; farmers and market-gardeners have blessed its abundant fertility; while industrialists have ruthlessly exploited its mineral resources. Not surprisingly, this is the region that Henry James described as 'the core and centre of the English world: midmost England, unmitigated England.'

In almost every corner of this enchanting countryside, with its smooth-rolling hills, fruit-laden orchards and dappled woodlands, can be found familiar names from the nation's past: Lady Godiva, immortalized for riding naked through the streets of Coventry; Guy of Warwick, the great legendary hero of medieval romance; Oliver Cromwell, who rose from the rank of captain at the Civil War battle of Edge Hill to become Lord Protector of the Commonwealth; Nell Gwynne, the Hereford-born orange-seller and actress who became Charles II's mistress; Charles II, who fled from the battle of Worcester and hid from the pursuing Parliamentarians in an oak tree at Boscobel; Sir Edward Elgar, born near Worcester in 1857 and the composer of the popular *Enigma Variations*, *The Dream of Gerontius* and the *Pomp and Circumstance* march; George Eliot, pseudonym of Mary Anne or Marian Evans, the Victorian novelist, who grew up in the countryside around Nuneaton; Dr Samuel Johnson, critic, poet, journalist and dictionary writer, who was born at Lichfield in 1709; Queen Elizabeth I, whose romantic association with Robert Dudley, Earl of Leicester, formed the basis of Sir Walter Scott's historical novel *Kenilworth*; Izaak Walton, a native of Stafford, renowned for *The Compleat Angler*, his great classic of angling literature, first published in 1653; and — towering above them all — William Shakespeare, revered throughout the English-speaking world as one of the greatest poets and dramatists of all time.

The names of the places associated with these distinguished figures are equally familiar: Stratford-upon-Avon, the world-famous market town where Shakespeare was born and died; Anne Hathaway's Cottage, the ancestral home of Shakespeare's wife; Mary Arden's House, the half-timbered farmhouse where the poet's mother lived before her marriage; Warwick Castle, one of the finest medieval fortresses in the realm; Coventry, a city which rose like the phoenix from the ashes of wartime destruction; Birmingham, Britain's second-largest city, with its origins firmly rooted in the industrial past; and the town of Rugby, famed for its public school and the origination of Rugby and American football.

The region also contains a tremendous variety of lesser-known but equally fascinating places: Charlecote Park, where the young Shakespeare was alleged to have been caught poaching deer; Royal Leamington Spa, with its wealth of Georgian, Regency and early Victorian architecture; the medieval, almost-islanded town of Shrewsbury, birthplace of Charles Darwin and the home of Ellis Peters' fictional detective and Benedictine monk, Brother Cadfael; Ironbridge, cradle of the Industrial Revolution; Hereford Cathedral, with its priceless Mappa Mundi, a unique thirteenth-century map of the world with Jerusalem at its centre; Viroconium, the sprawling remains of what was once the fourth largest city in Roman Britain; Witley Court, a palatial country mansion, once rivalling Blenheim in opulence, and now a spectacular ruin; and Offa's Dyke, the huge earthwork mound and ditch that marked the boundary between England and Wales during the Dark Ages.

Even to the stranger the towns and cities, villages and hamlets lying within this illustrious region seem curiously comfortable and familiar, not just because their virtues have been extolled by countless poets and writers but because they somehow encapsulate all that is best in the traditional English scene: quaint old-world cottages like those at Shottery, Welford-upon-Avon, Elmley Castle, Abbots Morton, and the Lenches; ancient churches, richly decorated with hallowed memorials of less materialistic times, like those at Kilpeck, Defford, Deerhurst, Melverley and Rochford; glorious cathedrals, show-pieces of towns like Gloucester, Worcester, Lichfield and Hereford; magnificent castles, reminders of a bygone feudal age, like Warwick, Ludlow, Goodrich, Bridgnorth, Whittington, Stafford, Tamworth and Kenilworth; stately mansions, the favoured homes of the aristocracy, like Shugborough Hall (Lord Lichfield), Compton Wynyates (Marquess of Northampton) and Ragley Hall (Earl of Yarmouth); historic manor houses, some moated, like Coughton Court, Packwood House, Baddesley Clinton, Stokesay Castle, Wightwick Manor and Lower Brockhampton; and once-great monastic houses, many of which were stripped of their treasures and sold or destroyed at the Dissolution, like those at Coombe, Buildwas, Abbey Dore, Haughmond, Tewkesbury, Pershore, Great and Little Malvern, Lilleshall, Evesham and Wenlock.

Prolific as the region is in literary, romantic and historical associations, the Heart of England is also noted for its immense rural charm and scenic beauty. Here, age-old rivers like the Avon, Severn, Wye and Teme meander lazily through emerald green fields and rich farmland to merge into the Bristol Channel and, eventually, the Atlantic Ocean. Isolated hills rise from the level plains like giant, slumbering prehistoric reptiles: the Wrekin, Bredon Hill and the Malvern Hills among the most prominent. Towards the Welsh border the flat landscape of the river valleys becomes rough and hilly, less populated and virtually forgotten. Here the main roads and motorways peter out to become quiet, narrow lanes and peaceful tracks. Amidst this timeless land of scattered farmsteads, remote rural communities and small market towns, the hills are studded with the long-neglected remnants of centuries of border warfare between ancient tribes, Romans and Britons, Normans and Welsh.

No ground in England has been the stage for so many tragic and dramatic events in the nation's long and turbulent history. In AD 50, somewhere amongst the sprawling hills close to the Welsh border, Caratacus made his last heroic stand against the might of the conquering Roman legions. Trapped within the loop of the river at Evesham on 4 August 1265, Simon de Montfort and his Barons' army met defeat and death at the hands of the Royalists under Prince Edward (later Edward I). At the battle of Shrewsbury on 21 July 1403, Sir Henry Percy (or Hotspur) was slain and his rebellious followers vanquished by the forces of Henry IV. During the Wars of the Roses, battles were fought at Mortimer's Cross (2 February 1461) and Tewkesbury (4 May 1471). The first major Civil War battle, between Royalists and Parliamentarians, occurred at Edge Hill on 23 October 1642. The last, at Worcester on 3 September 1651, saw the defeat of Charles II and the routing of his army. Major conflicts such as these have provided inspiration for countless poets and writers; none more notable than Shakespeare whose history plays, with scenes set in the locality, include *Henry IV*, *Richard II*, and *Henry VI*.

One of the earliest writers to have referred to the region, or more particularly his native Warwickshire, as the Heart of England was Michael Drayton, born at Hartshill in 1563. In his *Poly-Olbion* he sings: 'Upon the Midlands now th' industrious Muse doth fall; / That Shire which we the heart of England well may call.' The name was adopted in 1973 by the Heart of England Tourist Board (formerly the West Midlands Tourist Board) and was deemed to embrace the geographical middle-land counties of Shropshire, Staffordshire, Hereford and Worcester, Gloucestershire, Warwickshire and West Midlands.

For the purposes of this book, however, the area referred to as the Heart of England has been reduced in size and re-defined to embrace: the counties of Warwickshire, Hereford and Worcester, and Shropshire; the metropolitan county of West Midlands; the southern half of Staffordshire (the unique gardens at Biddulph Grange in the north, however, could not be ignored and are included); and the north-western corner of Gloucestershire, bounded in the south by an imaginary line from Symond's Yat to Gloucester and running north-east below the Cotswold escarpment to Cheltenham and Childswickham, near Broadway (Broadway, however, has not been included because it is featured in the authors' companion volume *The Cotswolds*). For administrative purposes the two counties of Herefordshire and Worcestershire were combined in 1974 to form the single large county of Hereford and Worcester, but because their character, history, geography and traditions are distinctly different, for this book it has been decided to revert to the pre-1974 boundaries and treat them as separate counties.

From the summits of many of the hills in the region there are extensive panoramas across the green and brown patchwork landscape of the flat river valleys, in some cases, embracing as many as fifteen counties. The scenic splendour of the view from Edge Hill at different times of the day was praised by Richard Jago in 1767. After celebrating the 'level plain, hills rising various, woods, / And meadows green, the simple cot and towns, / Nurseries of arts and commerce!', he draws attention to the 'still more distant scenes, with legends strange'; and urges 'attentive let us scan, and / All their charms and mysteries explore'. Happily, the exploration of the bountiful 'charms and mysteries' of the Heart of England still holds out an irresistibly tempting invitation.

St Mary's and St David's Church
Kilpeck

Standing on the site of a Saxon foundation, the church of SS Mary and David at Kilpeck was started after the Norman Conquest and completed by the mid-twelfth century. Pevsner calls it 'one of the most perfect village churches in England'. Built of red sandstone and decorated by the Herefordshire school of travelling masons, who also worked on Shobdon church, the building has withstood the weathering of over eight centuries remarkably well. It was restored in 1848 and boasts an astounding collection of Romanesque sculpture, the most striking being the portal and columns of the south doorway. West of the church, the Normans built a motte-and-bailey castle. It stood on the site of an earlier stronghold, established in the eighth century by Offa, King of Mercia, as one of a series of outposts in the defence of Hereford. Little remains of this Norman administrative centre of the district of Archenfield, except earthworks and fragments of the keep. Traces of the medieval village, which stood outside the castle and covered some 6 acres, can still be found. Kilpeck, with stone and timber-framed houses, is 9 miles south-west of Hereford.

Stratford-upon-Avon and Warwickshire

Anne Hathaway's Cottage
Shottery

In 1582, at the age of eighteen, William Shakespeare married Anne Hathaway, the daughter of Richard Hathaway, a well-respected yeoman farmer who lived in Shottery, a small hamlet a mile to the west of Stratford-upon-Avon. The Hathaway family lived in a spacious twelve-roomed farmhouse, originally called 'Hewlands Farm' but now known as Anne Hathaway's Cottage. The oldest part of the half-timbered building, with its irregular walls, high-pitched thatched roof, tall brick chimney stacks and tiny latticed windows, dates from the fifteenth century. The house was owned and occupied by descendants of the Hathaways until 1892, when it was purchased by the Shakespeare Birthplace Trustees. Many of the original furnishings still survive. Part of the house was damaged by fire in 1969 but has been carefully restored. The garden at the front is filled with traditional flowers, while at the back is an orchard and the Shakespeare tree garden. Born here in 1556, Anne gave birth to Susanna in 1583 and the twins Hamnet and Judith in 1585. She died in 1623.

John Leland, the antiquary, included the small market town of Stratford-upon-Avon in his *Itinerary*, written in or about the years 1535–43. 'The town of Stratford standeth upon a plain ground on the right hand or ripe of Avon, as the water descendeth. It hath 2 or 3 very large streets, beside back lanes. One of the principal streets leadeth from east to west, another from south to north. The town is reasonably well builded of timber.'

Some twenty or so years later, on 23 April 1564, in a half-timbered house in Henley Street William Shakespeare was born. Today Shakespeare and Stratford are synonymous. The poet attended the local grammar school, married Anne Hathaway at the age of eighteen and, after fathering Susanna and the twins Hamnet and Judith, left Stratford for reasons not definitely known. He can be traced in London from 1592, first as an actor and then as a reviser of plays. In 1597, with wealth from success as a writer and part-owner of the Globe Theatre, he purchased New Place in Stratford, a substantial property, described by Leland as 'a pretty house of brick and timber', with gardens and orchards running down to the banks of the Avon. It was at New Place, while celebrating his fifty-second birthday, reputedly with his friends Michael Drayton and Ben Jonson, that Shakespeare died. He was buried in the chancel of Holy Trinity Church on 25 April 1616. Such is the poet's standing today that each year on the anniversary of his birth and death, St George's Day, his grave is festooned with floral tributes from over a hundred countries around the world.

Mary Mackay (1855–1924), who wrote under the pseudonym Marie Corelli, is also buried at Stratford. She lived at Mason Croft from 1901 and is remembered, at least locally, for importing a full-size gondola from Venice and employing 'a swart and muscle-bound gondolier' to transport her up and down the Avon in it. The gondolier, who was often too drunk to take the helm, was dismissed after an argument in which he pulled out a knife. G. M. Trevelyan, the English historian, was born at Welcombe House in Stratford, now the Welcombe Hotel, in 1876.

Michael Drayton, celebrated for his long topographical poem *Poly-Olbion*, was born in 1563 in the north of the county at Hartshill, near Nuneaton. Although he died in comparative poverty, he was buried at Westminster Abbey in 1631 (his monument was paid for by Lady Anne Clifford, Countess of Dorset).

Born in 1819 on the Arbury estate in the parish of Chivers Coton, not far from

Drayton's birthplace, was Mary Ann Evans, better known as George Eliot. Much of her work draws inspiration from the years of her childhood, spent amongst the people and countryside of the Nuneaton district. Arbury Hall, where her father was employed as land agent, is, for example, the Cheverel Manor of *Mr Gilfil's Love-Story*, while the granite quarry of Griff Hollow, near Griff House (now a hotel), where she lived from 1820 to 1841, is the Red Deeps in *The Mill on the Floss*.

Richard Jago, born at Beaudesert, near Henley-in-Arden, in 1715 and incumbent of various Warwickshire parishes, is probably best known for his topographical poem *Edge-hill*, published in four books in 1767. Like Jago, William Shenstone (1714–63), the poet and essayist, went to school at Solihull. A native of Halesowen, Shenstone established his reputation with *The Judgement of Hercules* (1741) and *The School-mistress* (1742), but today his work has almost been forgotten. The young Samuel Johnson, born at Lichfield in 1709, unsuccessfully applied for the post of headmaster at Solihull School in 1735. The governors' report accepted that he was an excellent scholar, but noted that 'he has the character of being a very haughty, ill natured gent, and he has such a way of distorting his face (which though he cannot help it), we think it may affect some young lads.'

Rugby School, which became one of the foremost schools in the country under the headmastership of Dr Thomas Arnold, was immortalized in Thomas Hughes' *Tom Brown's Schooldays*. Among the writers educated at the school were: Charles Lutwidge Dodgson, better known as Lewis Carroll (1832–98); Matthew Arnold (1822–88), the eldest son of Dr Arnold; and the Rugby-born Rupert Brooke (1887–1915). Walter Savage Landor, born at Warwick in 1775, was expelled after insulting the headmaster in verse.

The number of distinguished poets and writers associated with the region is astonishing. Apart from those already mentioned, others include Izaak Walton, Chandos Leigh, Francis Brett Young, Samuel Butler, Charles Darwin, Benjamin Disraeli, William Hazlitt, A. E. Housman, William Langland, Philip Larkin, John Masefield, Ordericus Vitalis, Mary Webb, Wilfred Owen, Arnold Bennett and P. G. Wodehouse. Yet, beacon-like, it is pre-eminently Shakespeare who beckons literary pilgrims from 'the four-corners of the earth' to Stratford-upon-Avon, 'leafy Warwickshire' and the rich heartland of England.

Warwick Castle
Warwick

Warwick Castle, one of the finest medieval castles in England, stands on a sandstone cliff overlooking the River Avon. There was a fortress on the site in 914, erected by Ethelfleda, daughter of Alfred the Great, as protection against the Danes. The large mound inside the present castle is known as Ethelfleda's Mound. Shortly after the Conquest, the Normans replaced the fortress with a wooden motte-and-bailey castle, and in the twelfth and thirteenth centuries that in turn was replaced with one of stone. Guy's Tower and Caesar's Tower were erected in the fourteenth century. The castle, its outer walls protected by a waterless moat, never had a keep. The entrance, however, was defended by a gatehouse and barbican. Queen Elizabeth I was entertained at the castle by Ambrose Dudley, Earl of Warwick, in August 1572. The property fell into disrepair during the early seventeenth century, but was restored. It was purchased by Madame Tussaud's in 1978 and is now one of the country's most popular tourist attractions.

St George's Church
Lower Brailes

Located in the south-eastern corner of the county, between Banbury and Shipston-on-Stour, the ancient village of Brailes is divided into two: Upper and Lower Brailes. Between the thirteenth and sixteenth centuries it became an important market centre with almost 2,000 inhabitants. In its heyday it was probably the third largest township in the county, after Coventry and Warwick, and its former prosperity is reflected in the church of St George. Known as the 'Cathedral of the Feldon', the present structure dates from the fourteenth century, but contains traces of late Saxon or early Norman work. It was considerably altered, enlarged and restored over the centuries, particularly during Victorian times. The village also contains a Catholic church, built in 1726, and a Methodist chapel, built in 1863. Brailes Hill, over 760 feet high, overlooks the village and church and is topped by a clump of trees known as Highwall Spinney or Coppice, locally called Brailes Clump. The earthwork remains at Upper Brailes once formed part of a motte-and-bailey castle.

Farnborough Hall
Farnborough

East of Edge Hill and some 6 miles north of Banbury, Farnborough Hall has been the home of the Holbech family since 1684. The old manor house was remodelled by William Holbech between 1745 and 1750 in the Classical style of a Palladian villa, probably using designs by his friend Sanderson Miller, who lived at nearby Radway. The magnificent rococo plasterwork inside the house is by William Perritt of Yorkshire. The garden was landscaped in the 1740s and contains a long ornamental lake and a broad terraced walk, three-quarters-of-a-mile long, on which are two small buildings: the Ionic Temple and the Oval Pavilion. At the end of the terrace is a tall obelisk, erected in 1751. It collapsed in 1823, and was rebuilt. The panoramic view of Edge Hill from the end of the terrace is now somewhat marred by the M40, opened in 1991, the route of which cuts through the Warmington valley below the house. The house and 344 acres of parkland were given to the National Trust by Geoffrey Holbech in 1960.

Vale of the Red Horse
from Edge Hill

The first major encounter of the English Civil War took place in the level fields below Edge Hill on 23 October 1642. Fought between the opposing armies of King Charles I and Parliament, it lasted until nightfall and resulted in an estimated 1,500 dead and both sides claiming victory. On Christmas Eve, two months later, a spectral army was reputed to have re-enacted the battle; an account of which was published the following year by Thomas Jackson in a pamphlet entitled *A Great Wonder in Heaven Shewing The Late Apparitions and prodigious noyes of War and Battels, seen on Edge-Hill near Keinton in Warwickshire*. Since then others have felt that the battleground is haunted. Much of the site is now owned by the Ministry of Defence and is barred to the public. The Castle Inn, overlooking the battlefield, stands close to the spot where the King's standard was raised. The tower was built by Sanderson Miller in about 1746–7, while the inn, adjacent, is Victorian.

Chesterton Windmill
Chesterton

A prominent landmark for miles around, Chesterton Windmill was built in 1632 for Sir Edward Peyto and may have been designed by Inigo Jones, who was a friend of the family. It was described by William Field in 1815: 'Without the fliers, the mill, which is of a circular form, would resemble a large temple, of no graceful symmetry. The body is supported by six arches, with pilaster capitals; and beneath them, by ordinary wooden stairs, is the ascent to the interior. The mill is surmounted by a leaden dome, which revolves for the purpose of shifting the fliers affixed to it, as the state of the wind requires.' It is now in the care of Warwickshire County Council and is occasionally open to the public. The Peyto family lived in a mansion at Chesterton, built about 1650–60, but it was demolished in about 1802. The Roman Fosse Way passes within a mile of the depopulated village and on it, north-north-west of Windmill Farm, is the site of a Roman settlement.

Compton Wynyates
near Brailes

On Castle Hill, near Sherbourne, about 5 miles north-east of Stratford-upon-Avon, stood the castle of Fulbrook, overlooking the green meadows and woodland of the Avon valley. It was demolished in the reign of Henry VIII by Sir William Compton, who used the materials to embellish his mansion at Compton Wynyates, 12 miles to the south-east. Situated in a delightful wooded hollow, the mansion is considered by Pevsner to be 'the most perfect picture-book house of the Early Tudor decades, the most perfect in England in the specific picturesque'. It originally had a moat, but this was filled in after the Civil War (the battlements were also destroyed). The Compton family have held the manor since at least 1204. Described as 'a picture of rose-tinted restfulness', the house is now the private home of the 7th Marquess of Northampton and is not open to the public. Its once-celebrated topiary garden no longer exists.

Mary Arden's House
Wilmcote

Three miles north-west of Stratford-upon-Avon, in the ancient village of Wilmcote, is a large Tudor farmstead, once the ancestral home of the Ardens. In the mid-sixteenth century it was called 'Ashbyes' and belonged to Robert Arden, a prosperous yeoman farmer, who owned land not only at Wilmcote but also at Snitterfield. Today the property is named after his daughter Mary, who married John Shakespeare in 1557 and gave birth to William seven years later. Dating from the early sixteenth century, the timber-framed building was occupied until 1930, when it was acquired by the Shakespeare Birthplace Trust. Mary Arden's House is constructed from locally quarried blue-grey stone and timber from the nearby Forest of Arden, while its roof is covered with hand-made clay tiles. The barns and outbuildings at the rear of the house contain a fascinating collection of old farming implements and tools. The Shakespeare Countryside Museum extends to include the buildings of Glebe Farm, adjacent.

Shakespeare's Birthplace
Stratford-upon-Avon

William Shakespeare was born in this half-timbered house in Henley Street on 23 April 1564. Typical of the houses and shops of Shakespeare's Stratford, the building dates from the early sixteenth century. Although it is now detached, the Birthplace originally formed part of a continuous street frontage (the adjoining houses were demolished in 1857 to reduce the risk of fire). Shakespeare's father was a wool dealer and a maker of soft leather goods, and records show that he owned and occupied parts of the premises as early as 1552. At the time of William's birth, the property consisted of the family home and their shop and warehouse. Despite repairs and alterations over the years, the building is basically original and its appearance exactly the same as the first known drawing of 1769. In 1847 it was sold by public auction and purchased as a national memorial, now administered by the Shakespeare Birthplace Trust.

New Place and Guild Chapel
Stratford-upon-Avon

New Place, one of the largest houses in Stratford, was built at the end of the fifteenth century by Hugh Clopton, who became Lord Mayor of London in 1492. Although Shakespeare purchased the property in 1597 with money achieved from success as a playwright in London, it was not until 1610 that he settled there permanently. Six years later, on 23 April, the poet died in the house, reputedly after drinking with Ben Jonson and Michael Drayton. In 1759, after a quarrel with the town authorities, the bad-tempered owner, the Reverend Francis Gastrell, pulled the building down and was subsequently driven out of the town by the enraged inhabitants. All that now remains are the foundations. One of the most attractive features of New Place is the replica of an Elizabethan Knott Garden, enclosed by a wooden palisade covered with crab-apple trees. Entrance to the site is via Nash's House, next door, which was the home of Shakespeare's granddaughter, Elizabeth, who married Thomas Nash in 1626. The medieval Guild Chapel, Grammar School and Alms Houses are immediately adjacent.

Hall's Croft
Stratford-upon-Avon

In 1607 Shakespeare's daughter Susanna married Dr John Hall, one of the town's leading physicians, who lived in this half-timbered, many gabled house in Old Town, near Holy Trinity Church. One of the finest surviving Elizabethan houses in Stratford, Hall's Croft now belongs to the Shakespeare Birthplace Trust and contains a fascinating and valuable collection of Tudor and Jacobean furniture. One room is furnished in the style of an Elizabethan consulting room, complete with herbals for reference, decorative pharmacy jars and pill pots, pestles and mortars and surgical instruments in use at the time. In his case-book, which details the herbs he prescribed for his patients, Dr Hall also entered the treatment he gave his wife. Shakespeare visited the house many times, but it is not known whether he was one of Dr Hall's patients. The spacious walled garden, with large lawn, ancient mulberry tree and herbaceous borders, was laid out after the restoration of the house in 1950.

Holy Trinity Church
Stratford-upon-Avon

William Shakespeare died on 23 April 1616, his fifty-second birthday. Two days later, he was buried in the chancel of Holy Trinity Church on the banks of the River Avon. Inscribed on the stone that marks his grave there is a curse, said to have been written by himself:

Good Frend for Jesus Sake Forebeare
To Digg the Dust Encloased Heare.
Blest Be ye Man yt Spares thes Stones
And Curst be He yt Moves My Bones.

Despite various attempts to have his body exhumed, the poet's bones have never been moved. Buried nearby are his wife, his daughter Susanna, her husband Dr John Hall and Thomas Nash. A short distance upstream from the church stands the Royal Shakespeare Theatre, completed in 1932 after the original theatre had been destroyed by fire in 1926. The Swan Theatre adjoining it was the gift of an anonymous benefactor and was officially opened by Queen Elizabeth II in November 1986.

Charlecote Park
Charlecote

According to tradition, young William Shakespeare was caught red-handed poaching deer from Charlecote Park, a few miles east of Stratford-upon-Avon. He was hauled before Sir Thomas Lucy, who was not only the lord of the manor but also a magistrate. Because of this unfortunate incident, it is said, Shakespeare fled to London. Later, as an act of revenge, he caricatured Sir Thomas as Justice Shallow in *The Merry Wives of Windsor* and thereby made him the laughing stock of London's playhouses. The Lucy family have lived at Charlecote since the end of the twelfth century. The present house was built in 1558 by Sir Thomas Lucy and designed in the shape of a capital 'E', in honour of Queen Elizabeth I. Like the main house, the gatehouse (built in 1550) is constructed of mellow rose-pink brick from the kilns at nearby Hampton Lucy. The grounds were landscaped by Lancelot 'Capability' Brown in 1760 and the mansion altered and extended between 1826 and 1867. The property was granted to the National Trust in 1946.

Hampton Lucy
from Charlecote Park

The village of Hampton Lucy lies on the west bank of the River Avon at the edge of Charlecote Park. Before the Dissolution it was owned by the Bishops of Worcester and was called Bishop's Hampton. Its name was changed to Hampton Lucy after the manor had been granted to the Lucy family of Charlecote in 1557. The church of St Peter was built by the Reverend John Lucy in 1826 and the former church demolished. Designed by Thomas Rickman, it is considered to be one of the earliest and best examples of the Gothic Revival. The iron bridge, spanning the Avon, was erected in 1829 by the Rev. Lucy and was cast at the Horseley Ironworks in Shropshire. It is said that Lucy, who was noted for his grand dinner parties, decided to build the bridge after many of his guests were unable to cross the river due to the unreliable state of the previous wooden bridges, which kept getting washed away. Charlecote Mill, nearby, dates from the eighteenth century. It closed during the 1950s but has been restored as a working corn mill.

St James's Church
Snitterfield

John Shakespeare, the poet's father, was born of farming stock in the hillside village of Snitterfield, some 4 miles north of Stratford-upon-Avon. He moved to Stratford some time before 1552, married Mary Arden of Wilmcote in 1557, held the office of High Bailiff in 1568, and was elected Chief Alderman in 1571. John's parents worshipped at the church of St James the Great, and almost certainly John and his brother Henry were baptized in the existing octagonal stone font with its circle of eight carved heads. Henry, Shakespeare's uncle, farmed at Snitterfield as a tenant of Hales Manor from 1574 to his death in December 1596. He and his wife Margaret (who died in February 1597) were buried somewhere in the churchyard. Dating from the thirteenth century, the church stands on the site of an earlier Norman or Saxon foundation. It was largely remodelled in mid-Victorian times. Richard Jago, born at Beaudesert, near Henley-in-Arden, in 1715, was vicar of the parish from 1754 to 1781. He is best remembered for his topographical poem *Edge-hill*, published in 1767.

Welcombe Hills
Stratford-upon-Avon

The Welcombe Hills, immediately north of Stratford-upon-Avon, were described by William Field in 1815 as 'a range of proudly swelling mounts, covered for the most part with tufted verdure, adorned with fine trees, some clustered together, others scattered about.' These uplands, now mainly under cultivation, are reputed to have been the site of a fierce battle between the Britons and the Saxons. It is said that the extensive entrenchments known as the Dingles were created by the soldiers to cover up the bodies of those who were slain. The hills were owned by the Clopton family, the lords of the manor, from the thirteenth to the eighteenth century. Hugh Clopton, who became Lord Mayor of London in 1492, built Clopton Bridge across the River Avon at Stratford in about 1485. With wealth from success in London, Shakespeare invested in land at Welcombe. The 120-foot-high granite obelisk on the summit was erected in 1876 by Robert Philips in memory of his brother Mark, a Manchester cotton manufacturer, who lived in the nearby Victorian mansion, now known as the Welcombe Hotel.

St Laurence's Church
Bidford-on-Avon

The village of Bidford-on-Avon stands on an old Roman road, known as Ryknild Street to the north and Buckle Street to the south. Here the River Avon is spanned by an eight-arched bridge, built in the fifteenth century. The ford, which it replaced, was situated near the church of St Laurence. The diversion of the road over the bridge 200 yards downstream may account for the lop-sided layout of the village. This consists of a single street, with the earliest buildings standing near the church and ford. The largest, the former Falcon Inn, dates from the sixteenth century. There is a tradition that William Shakespeare, among a party from Stratford, challenged the locals at Bidford to a drinking contest at the Falcon. The poet and his companions were beaten. The following morning, when urged to renew the contest, Shakespeare is said to have replied: 'No! I have had enough. I have drunk with

Piping Pebworth, dancing
  Marston,
Haunted Hillborough, hungry
  Grafton,
Dodging Exhall, papish Wixford,
Beggarly Broom, and drunken
  Bidford.'

Boat Lane
Welford-on-Avon

The ancient village of Welford is surrounded by extensive modern housing developments. Yet the area near the church of St Peter, including Boat Lane, still retains a number of black-and-white timber-framed thatched cottages. The Four Alls public house is said to take its name from: 'A king who rules over all; a parson who prays for all; a soldier who fights for all; and a farmer who pays for all.' At the southern end of the village is a maypole, some 65 feet tall and spirally painted red, white and blue. The church records contain a vivid account of the Avon in flood on 18 July 1588. The rising water apparently destroyed Grange Mill, houses in Warwick, and both ends of Stratford Bridge. It filled the fishpool at Welford parsonage, took away the signpost at The Bear and carried away Edward Butler's cart. 'It drowned three furlongs of corn in Welford field. It was so high at the height that it unthatched the mill . . . and did take away one Sale's daughters of Grafton, out of Hillborough meadow . . .'

Ragley Hall
Alcester

The home of the Earl and Countess of Yarmouth, Ragley Hall was designed in 1680 by Robert Hooke for the Earl of Conway and replaced a medieval embattled castle. The Great Hall, with its magnificent baroque plasterwork, was designed by James Gibbs in 1750. James Wyatt's additions during the 1780s included the Ionic portico on the East Front and the circular stable block. Brewer wrote in 1814: 'This fine residence is situated on a commanding elevation, and is of noble size and proportions. The building is three stories high, and displays four fronts, each of which is conspicuous for architectural beauty. The spacious interior is well adapted to purposes of state and pleasure. The entrance hall is of grand proportions, and is embellished with much fine stucco work.' The huge mural on the walls and ceiling of the South Staircase Hall was completed by Graham Rust in 1983. The Palladian mansion is surrounded by 400 acres of wooded parkland, originally laid out by Capability Brown in the 1750s.

Malt Mill Lane
Alcester

At the confluence of the rivers Arrow and Alne, the small town of Alcester also stands at the meeting point of two Roman roads, one of which is Ryknild Street. It is an ancient settlement, pre-dating even the Romans who occupied a station at the site, probably Alauna. Of the moated Benedictine monastery, known as 'The Church of Our Lady of the Isle', founded to the north of the town in 1140, nothing remains. During medieval times Alcester was a busy iron-working centre, later manufacturing needles. Most of the buildings today date from the sixteenth to eighteenth century. The oldest house in the town is the half-timbered Old Malt House in Malt Mill Lane, off Church Street. It was built in 1500. The Town Hall, erected in about 1620–40, was once a market hall with an open colonnade on the ground floor. The red-brick-fronted Churchill House, opposite, is dated 1688. The church of St Nicholas dates from the late thirteenth century, but was largely rebuilt in 1870–71.

Coughton Court
near Alcester

The Throckmortons first came to Coughton Court in 1409. Devout and tenacious Roman Catholics, they were involved in the 1583 plot to murder Elizabeth I and place Mary Queen of Scots on the English throne in her stead. They were also indirectly involved in the Gunpowder Plot of 1605. During the Civil War the family were staunchly Royalist and in 1643 the house was besieged and occupied by Parliamentary forces. In 1688, after the flight of James II, a Protestant mob from Alcester sacked the house and destroyed the east wing together with the chapel. It was never rebuilt. The great gatehouse was erected in about 1509, while the stone-built Gothic wings on either side were added in 1780. The house is, however, essentially Elizabethan and was formerly moated, but this was drained and filled in 1795. Although the estate was given to the National Trust in 1945, it remains the Warwickshire home of the family. The name Coughton is derived from the family of de Cocton, who originally owned the manor.

Packwood House
near Hockley Heath

Some 2 miles west of Baddesley Clinton, Packwood House was built in about 1560, with mid-seventeenth-century and twentieth-century additions. Essentially timber-framed, the exterior has now been rendered over. On the south side of the house is a delightful sunken garden, known as the Carolean Garden. In each corner is a gazebo; the one in the north-east corner contains a fireplace, chimney and horizontal flue to warm fruit trees ripening on the adjacent wall. The famous Yew Garden, beyond, was first laid out in the seventeenth century by John Fetherston. It is traditionally said to represent the Sermon on the Mount. Twelve of the trees stand for the Apostles, while four larger trees in the middle symbolize the Evangelists. The Mount is crowned by a single yew, representing 'The Master'. The Fetherston family lived in the house until 1869. The estate was given to the National Trust in 1941 by Graham Baron Ash, together with his valuable collection of furniture, tapestries and works of art.

George House
Henley-in-Arden

The ancient manorial town of Henley-in-Arden, built essentially along one main street, lies (together with Beaudesert) in the shelter of the hill called The Mount, some 9 miles west of Warwick. Among the houses of note are: the Elizabethan Guildhall, by the church of St John Baptist; the timber-framed inn, The Blue Bell, dating from the fifteenth and sixteenth centuries; the seventeenth-century White Swan Hotel, formerly a coaching inn and much restored; and, near the remains of the old market cross, the sixteenth-century George House, formerly the Old George, with 'phoney trimmings', according to Pevsner. St Nicholas's church at Beaudesert, on the opposite side of the River Alne, dates from about 1170. Its cemetery climbs up the western side of The Mount, on the summit of which are the earthwork remains of a motte-and-bailey castle, built by the Norman Thurstan de Montfort towards the end of the eleventh century. Richard Jago, the poet, was born at Beaudesert in 1715. His father, Richard, was vicar of the church from 1709 to 1741.

Baddesley Clinton
near Hockley Heath

The medieval manor house of Baddesley Clinton, its moat dating from the thirteenth century, stands in ancient parkland, some 7 miles north-west of Warwick. It was established amidst the Forest of Arden shortly after the Norman Conquest, when Geoffrey de Wirce was granted the manor by William I. After Wirce's death it reverted to the Crown and subsequently passed through many ownerships until it became the property of John Brome of Warwick in 1438. His son, Nicholas, rebuilt the east and west ranges. The house was extensively remodelled in the late sixteenth and seventeenth century by Henry Ferrers 'the Antiquary', whose father had married Nicholas's daughter. Construction, which included rebuilding most of the south range, adding corridors to the west range and creating the Great Parlour, was completed by Ferrers' son Edward. The Ferrers family lived in the house until 1939. It was purchased by the government in 1980, and the ownership was transferred to the National Trust.

Warwick Castle
Warwick

During the Middle Ages, Warwick was by far the most famous of all the castles of the Midlands and the exploits of its powerful earls were renowned throughout the realm. Earls of Warwick have been involved in most of the influential events in the nation's history. They were prominent in the wars of Stephen and Edward II, the Hundred Years' War, the Wars of the Roses and the Civil War. They fought on the side of the monarchs, and they also fought against them. In 1312 Guy de Beauchamp, the tenth earl, was influential in the trial and execution of Edward II's favourite, Piers Gaveston. Richard Beauchamp, the thirteenth earl and trusted friend of Henry V, superintended the trial and execution of Joan of Arc in 1431. Richard Neville, his successor, was known as 'The Kingmaker' because of his power and influence in the struggle for the crown during the Wars of the Roses. Ambrose Dudley, the twenty-first earl, was party to the execution of Mary, Queen of Scots, in 1587. In 1618 the title Earl of Warwick was conferred on Robert, Lord Rich. The castle, however, was given to the Greville family in 1604, who were later granted the title Earl of Warwick. It remains with them to this day.

Lord Leycester's Hospital
Warwick

In about 1540 John Leland wrote of Warwick in his *Itinerary*: 'The beauty and glory of the town is in two streets, whereof the one is called the High Street, and goeth from the east gate to the west, having a right goodly cross in the middle of it. The other crosseth the middle of it, making Quadrivium, and goeth from north to south.' Two hundred and fifty houses in the town were destroyed by fire in 1694. St Mary's church was badly damaged but fortunately the magnificent Beauchamp Chapel, built in 1443–64, survived. A number of other buildings escaped the conflagration, including Lord Leycester's Hospital founded by Robert Dudley, Earl of Leicester, in 1571. It stands beside the narrow West Gate of the town, above which is the Chapel of St James. The Hospital is centred around a small courtyard notable for its rich gables, ornamented by the arms of families connected with Dudley. It continues to provide accommodation for ex-servicemen, who on occasions can be seen wearing their traditional Elizabethan dress. It also houses the Regimental Museum of the Queen's Own Hussars.

Lansdowne Circus
Royal Leamington Spa

In addition to its parks and gardens, Royal Leamington Spa is memorable for its broad tree-lined avenues, white-painted terraces, and wealth of Georgian, Regency and early Victorian architecture. During the 1830s William Thomas designed a series of attractive residences in the town, including Lansdowne Crescent, with its delicately fretted iron verandas, and Lansdowne Circus, a small cul-de-sac of classical houses built in pairs, also with verandas. Nathaniel Hawthorne, the American novelist, stayed at 10 Lansdowne Circus. In *Our Old Home*, published in 1863, he called it 'one of the coziest nooks in England or in the world'. He added: 'The modest abode to which I have alluded forms one of a circular range of pretty, moderate-sized, two-story houses, all built on nearly the same plan, and each provided with its little grass plot, its flowers, its tufts of box trimmed into globes and other fantastic shapes, and its verdant hedges shutting the house in from the common drive, and dividing it from its equally cozy neighbors.'

Guy's Cliffe
near Leamington Spa

The dark, mysterious shell of what was once an impressive Georgian mansion stands on the top of a high sandstone cliff overlooking the River Avon at Guy's Cliffe, near Warwick. It was built in about 1751 for Samuel Greatheed. Sarah Siddons the actress became a maid in the house in 1772. In 1826 the property descended to the Percy family, who held it until 1946, when it was sold and allowed to fall into decay. The historian John Rous, who was chaplain of the chapel here until his death in 1491, states that St Dubricius established an oratory on the site, dedicated to St Mary Magdalen. It is thought that this occurred in the mid-sixth century AD. The spot became a favoured haunt for hermits, who occupied caves carved out of the soft sandstone rock. At the foot of the cliff, beside the river, is a large but shallow cave named after Guy of Warwick, one of the great heroes of medieval romance. It was here, according to legend, that he died in the arms of his wife, Felice.

Kenilworth Castle
Kenilworth

Queen Elizabeth I granted Kenilworth Castle to her favourite courtier Robert Dudley, Earl of Leicester, in 1563. She visited him at the castle on a number of occasions, but the most memorable was her visit of 1575 which lasted a total of seventeen days. No expense was spared in the festivities. Sir Walter Scott based his novel *Kenilworth*, published in 1821, on the relationship between the Queen and the Earl, and the tragic fate of Amy Robsart, the Earl's wife. Gossip suggested that she had been murdered by Dudley so that he would be free to marry Elizabeth. The castle at this time was surrounded by a vast defensive lake, half a mile long and a quarter of a mile wide. In 1642, after the Battle of Edge Hill, the castle was seized by the Parliamentarians and, at the end of the Civil War, Parliament ordered its destruction. The lake was drained, but the fortress was only partially demolished. The ruins were given to the nation in 1937 and are now in the care of English Heritage.

Coombe Abbey
near Coventry

The Cistercian abbey at Coombe was founded by Richard de Camville in 1150. By the end of the thirteenth century it had become the wealthiest and most powerful religious house in the county. The following century, however, it was heavily in debt due to the defective rule of Abbot Richard, who took over the office in 1328. After the Dissolution in 1539, the abbey was partially demolished and the structures that remained were used for living accommodation. In 1581 the property passed, by marriage, to Sir John Harington whose two-storeyed house, built partly of stone and partly of wood, incorporated parts of the old monastery buildings. The estate belonged to the Craven family from 1622 until 1923. A new west front, designed by William Winde, was added between 1680 and 1691. In about 1771 the grounds and surrounding parkland were landscaped by Capability Brown. Coventry Corporation acquired the estate between 1953 and 1964 and it is now known as Coombe Abbey Country Park. Throughout the year medieval banquets are staged in the moated house.

Skep Cottage
Stoneleigh

Situated on rising ground on the western bank of the River Sowe, near its confluence with the Avon, is the ancient village of Stoneleigh. Formerly a river-crossing settlement, deep in the Forest of Arden, it was a royal manor until 1154, when Henry II granted the land to a small community of Cistercian monks. After the Dissolution Stoneleigh Abbey was granted to Charles Brandon, Duke of Suffolk, and in 1561 it was sold to Sir Rowland Hill and Sir Thomas Leigh. On Hill's death the property passed, by marriage, to Sir Thomas, remaining in the family for the next 400 years. The village contains a pleasing variety of stone, red-brick and timber-framed buildings. The oldest house is possibly the mid-fifteenth-century Skep Cottage. Of cruck-frame construction, the western end was rebuilt in the seventeenth century. In the centre of the village, sited on a raised green under the shade of a large chestnut tree, is a blacksmith's forge, dated 1851. Overlooking the parish church and the sloping meadows and woods of the Sowe Valley is the black-and-white, timber-framed Manor Farmhouse. The Royal Show is held annually in the grounds of the National Agricultural Centre, Stoneleigh.

Rugby School
Rugby

The busy industrial town of Rugby, situated on a plateau south of the River Avon, dates back to Saxon times and was recorded in the Norman survey of 1086 as Rocheberie. It is most noted for its public school, founded in 1567 by Lawrence Sheriff of nearby Brownsover. A new school was built in the mid-eighteenth century and by 1783 all vestiges of the original schoolhouse had been demolished. It became one of the foremost schools in the country under Dr Thomas Arnold (headmaster from 1828 to 1842), who is featured in *Tom Brown's Schooldays* by Thomas Hughes, published in 1857. Just prior to this period, according to a granite plaque (shown in the photograph), a boy named William Webb Ellis 'with a fine disregard for the rules of football as played in his time first took the ball in his arms and ran with it thus originating the distinctive feature of the Rugby game. A.D. 1823.' Among the famous men educated at the school were Matthew Arnold, C. L. Dodgson (Lewis Carroll), Rupert Brooke and Walter Savage Landor.

Birmingham and the West Midlands

Coventry
from Knightlow Hill

Some say the name 'Coventry' is derived from 'convent town', after the seventh-century foundation of a convent or nunnery by St Osburg, built on high ground in a clearing in the Forest of Arden. Others argue, however, that the name is derived from the tree of a person named Cofa. The convent was destroyed by the Danes in 1016, and in 1043 Earl Leofric founded a Benedictine monastery on the site. In 1086, at the time of the Norman survey, Coventry was a small farming community. By the end of the fourteenth century it had become the fourth largest city in England and the midland centre of the woollen cloth industry. It was also noted for the production of caps, soap, needles and leather goods. At the height of its prosperity the city was enclosed by a wall, over 2 miles in length. It was demolished in 1662 on the orders of Charles II, although parts of it still remain. Among the medieval buildings to survive are Bablake School, Bond's Hospital, Ford's Hospital, St John's Hospital and St Mary's Guildhall. Coventry became a major car manufacturing centre after Daimler opened a factory in 1896.

During Saxon times Birmingham was little more than a clearing in the great forest of Arden, probably belonging to the family of Beorma or Beornmund, from whom it takes its name. In 1086, according to the Domesday Book, it was a tiny hamlet, valued at twenty shillings (or one pound), with five villagers and four smallholders. Originally sited on the southern slope of a sandstone ridge above the River Rea, Birmingham slowly developed into a thriving medieval market town, with a moated manor house located near the present Bull Ring. The parish church of St Martin dates from Norman times but was rebuilt in the late thirteenth century. By the nineteenth century the church was in such a bad state of repair that in 1873–5 it was carefully demolished, except for the tower and spire, and rebuilt in the style of the early fourteenth century. Inside the smoke-blackened building are several memorials to the de Bermingham family, who were lords of the manor in the fourteenth and fifteenth centuries.

Leland visited the town in about 1540 and wrote:

> The beauty of Bremischam, a good market town in the extreme parts that way of Warwickshire, is in one street going up along almost from the left ripe of the brook up a mean hill by the length of a quarter of a mile. I saw but one parish church in the town. There be many smiths in the town that use to make knives and all manner of cutting tools, and many lorimers that make bits, and a great many nailers. So that a great part of the town is maintained by smiths. The smiths there have iron out of Staffordshire and Warwickshire and sea-coal out of Staffordshire.

Some fifty years later, Camden noted that the place was 'swarming with inhabitants, and echoing with the noise of anvils, (for here are great numbers of smiths)'.

The rapid expansion of Birmingham, from a small market town to the second largest city in Britain, was due entirely to the skill, energy and ingenuity of its craftsmen, principally iron- and metal-workers, and the goods they manufactured. In 1586 the population numbered about 1,500. One hundred years later, this figure had more than doubled, due to the massive demand for sword blades to pursue the Civil War. Yet, in the 200 years from the beginning of the eighteenth century, the population jumped from 15,000 to over half a million. The French sociologist and historian, Alexis de Tocqueville, summed up the distinctive character of the town in 1835: 'It is an immense workshop, a huge forge, a vast shop. One only sees busy people and faces brown with smoke. One hears nothing but the sound of hammers and the whistle of steam escaping from boilers.'

Variously called the 'Town of a Thousand Trades' and the 'Workshop of the World', Birmingham's dramatic rise to prominence can be directly linked to the Industrial Revolution which originated some 28 miles to the north-west, in Coalbrookdale, Shropshire. For years, blast furnaces in the vicinity had used charcoal to smelt raw iron-ore, mined on the edge of the Shropshire coalfield. Dwindling supplies of timber, however, limited production and encouraged the importation of iron from overseas. Early attempts to smelt iron using coal – which was available in enormous quantities in the West Midlands, east Shropshire, north Warwickshire and Staffordshire, and specifically in the area north and west of Birmingham (later called the Black Country) – met with little success. The breakthrough, however, came in 1709 when the Quaker ironmaster, Abraham Darby 1, discovered a method of using coke to smelt iron and heralded a revolution in large-scale industrial production that was to sweep through the Western world.

In 1862 Randall wrote about the Severn Valley:

Francis Horner truly observes 'iron is the soul of every other manufacture, and the main-spring of civilized society.' It forms the heaviest shot, the largest gun, and the sharpest lancet. It makes the most elastic spring, the heaviest hammer, the longest wire, and the greatest ship. In the trembling needle out at sea, in the palace of glass at Sydenham, in the steel pen, in the tubular bridge and in railways; in numerous castings, ornamental and useful, for the palace or the cot – are witnessed the wonderful modifications of which it is susceptible.

Surrounded by seemingly inexhaustible supplies of iron and coal and at the hub and geographical centre of England's inland waterway system, Birmingham flourished as a manufacturing town, especially in metalwork. At its peak, tens of thousands of craftsmen turned their forges and workshops to the production of everything from buttons to guns, from jewellery to steam engines, and from candlesticks to wire. Products stamped 'Made in Birmingham' came to be recognized by almost every country in the world for their quality and reliability.

Since the Second World War, much of the city centre has been rebuilt with ring roads, shopping malls and tall office blocks. And today, Birmingham is fast gaining an international reputation as one of Britain's leading cultural, conference and exhibition centres, actively promoted as 'The Big Heart of England'.

Dudley Castle
Dudley

At the time of the Domesday survey of 1086 Dudley Castle was held by William FitzAnsculf, whose father was granted the estate of Dudley in about 1070. The timber motte-and-bailey fortress was replaced with a stone castle during the early twelfth century by the de Paganel family, who came into the estate, probably by marriage. Although it withstood a siege by King Stephen in 1138, the castle was destroyed in 1175 by Henry II. The property was inherited by Ralph de Somery in 1194. Because of his support in suppressing the rebellion of Simon de Montfort, Henry III granted Roger de Somery the right to restore the castle in 1264. Building continued into the following century and the gatehouse, keep and most of the curtain walls survive from this period. Further additions and restorations were carried out over the centuries. During the fourteenth century, the castle passed by marriage to the Suttons, who later adopted the name of Dudley. In 1643 the castle came into the ownership of the Ward family. It was partly demolished in 1647 during the Civil War and, after being gutted by fire in 1750, it was abandoned.

Coventry Cathedral
Coventry

In 1642 Nehemiah Wharton described Coventry as 'a city invironed with a wall coequal, if not exceeding that of London for breadth and height; the compass of it near 3 miles' with 'four strong gates, strong battlements . . . sweet and pleasant springs of water . . . magnificent churches and stately streets . . . very sweetly situate.' Three hundred years later, the German air raids of the Second World War left the city in ruins and the old Cathedral Church of St Michael a gutted shell. Undaunted, Coventry rose, like the phoenix, from the ashes of wartime destruction to become a brand new city with an inner ring road, office blocks and high-rise flats, housing zones, industrial estates, a traffic-free shopping centre with covered walkways and another cathedral to replace the one that was destroyed in the blitz. In pride of place, in the centre of Broadgate, was erected a bronze statue of Lady Godiva on horseback and, in a niche above one of the precincts, a painted effigy of 'Peeping Tom'. The legend of Lady Godiva, who rode naked through the city to force her husband Leofric, Earl of Mercia, to reduce the taxes, is based on historical fact. Peeping Tom, however, is a later embellishment.

Selly Manor
Bournville

In 1879 George and Richard Cadbury, cocoa and chocolate manufacturers, moved their factory from the heart of Birmingham to a rural site 4 miles to the south-west. Shortly after, close to the works, they built a few semi-detached houses for key workers. After the purchase in 1893 of 120 acres of land adjoining the factory, George Cadbury began to develop his new village of Bournville (named after the nearby Bournbrook), designed to provide better housing for all sections of the working community. In 1907, hearing that the timber-framed 'Rookery Cottages', in Bournbrook Road, were in the way of his new development, Cadbury decided to rescue the 600-year-old building from demolition. In 1912–16 the house was carefully dismantled, re-erected and restored to the condition it would have looked like in late Tudor times. 'Rookery Cottages' – essentially three labourer's dwellings – thereafter reverted to its former name of Selly Manor, and was opened to the public on 17 September 1917. Soon afterwards, it was placed in the care of the Bournville Village Trust, who now not only maintain and run the house, but also look after the 1,000-acre Bournville estate.

Birmingham Cathedral
Birmingham

Designed by Thomas Archer in English Baroque style and built between 1709 and 1715, the parish church of St Philip became the cathedral of the newly created diocese of Birmingham in 1905. It stands in the heart of the city centre, surrounded by high office buildings, most of which are Victorian. The stone, which came from quarries at Umberslade in Warwickshire, suffered badly from weathering, and the exterior had to be refaced in 1864–9 by J. A. Chatwin. The tower, completed in 1725, was refaced in 1958–9. The four large and vibrant stained glass windows (three in the east and one in the west) are by Edward Burne-Jones and depict the Ascension of Christ, His Birth (the Nativity), His Crucifixion and Doom (the Last Judgement). They were erected in 1884, 1887, 1887 and 1897, respectively. Burne-Jones, who was born in Birmingham on 28 August 1833, was baptized in the church on 1 January 1834. In the churchyard is a bronze statue of Charles Gore, first Bishop of Birmingham, made by Stirling Lee in 1914. Close by is a small stone in memory of Nanetta Stoker, who died in 1819. It seems that she was only 33 inches high.

The Council House
Birmingham

The most prominent building in Victoria Square is the Council House, designed in the Italian Renaissance style by Yeoville Thomason and built between 1874 and 1879. Within the central arch is a mosaic by Salviati. The gabled pediment above contains a representation of Britannia rewarding the manufacturers of Birmingham. Joseph Chamberlain, Liberal MP, businessman and mayor of Birmingham, laid the foundation stone in 1874. The nearby clock tower, 160 feet high, is known locally as Big Brum. To the west of the square is the Town Hall, designed by J. A. Hansom and E. Welch and modelled on the Temple of Castor and Pollux in the Roman Forum. Built of brick and faced with Anglesey marble, construction started in 1832 but was halted two years later when the builders were declared bankrupt. It was finished under the supervision of Charles Edge, a local architect, who remained in charge until 1861. The bronze statue of Queen Victoria, unveiled by Princess Margaret in 1951, is a recasting of the original erected in 1901.

Black Country Museum
Dudley

An open-air complex centred around buildings, transport and machinery, the Black Country Museum was established in 1975 to preserve something of the history and way of life of the people of the industrial Black Country. The Village, the heart of the museum, depicts living and working conditions in the late nineteenth and twentieth centuries. The shops, houses, cottages and workshops have either been transferred from their original site or been built to a traditional design. The street in the photograph shows the properties in which the poorest people would have lived. It contains a small row of cottages, based on an existing row in Station Road, Old Hill, dating from the late eighteenth century. The low building adjacent is a replica of a nailmaker's shop from Halesowen. At the far end of the street is the Bottle and Glass public house, behind which runs the Dudley Canal. The Methodist Chapel opposite was originally built in 1837 at Darby Hand, Netherton. It was dismantled and re-assembled on its present site between 1977 and 1979. Further displays include a canal boat dock, a steam engine, lime kilns, a colliery, underground mining and a travelling fairground.

Wightwick Manor
near Wolverhampton

Samuel Theodore Mander, a Wolverhampton paint and varnish manufacturer, purchased the Old Manor of Wightwick in 1887 and commissioned Edward Ould of Chester to build a new house beside it. Ould produced a pseudo-medieval house of striking design, with gables, Ruabon brickwork, decorative black-and-white oak timbering and carving by Edward Griffiths. The east wing, built in 1893, with tall spiral chimneys, is clearly influenced by the richly decorated Tudor buildings of the Welsh Marches. Wightwick Manor is particularly noted for its collection of furnishings by Morris and Company, a firm founded by William Morris and inspired by the ideas of Ruskin and the Pre-Raphaelites. In addition to Morris textiles, wallpapers and carpets, William de Morgan tiles, and W. A. S. Benson metalwork, the Mander family collected drawings and paintings by numerous artists belonging or allied to the Pre-Raphaelite brotherhood; notably Burne-Jones, Ruskin, Dante Gabriel Rossetti, Holman Hunt, and J. E. Millais. The gardens were laid out by Alfred Parsons in 1887 and Thomas Mawson in 1910. The property was given to the National Trust in 1937.

Lichfield and Staffordshire

The Sheepwalks
from Kinver Edge

At the southernmost tip of Staffordshire, 4 miles north of Kidderminster, is a prominent sandstone escarpment known as Kinver Edge. Consisting of high heath and woodland, self-seeded by birch, oak and pine, much of the ridge is in the care of the National Trust. Kingsford Country Park, owned by Hereford and Worcester County Council, forms the southern part of the Edge. Traces of an Iron Age hill-fort can be found on the promontory overlooking Kinver village. At Holy Austin Rock (below the fort), Vale's or Crow's Rock (in Kingsford Country Park), and Nanny's Rock (midway along the Edge) people lived in houses hollowed out of the soft sandstone rock. The last of these rock-dwellers, some of whom made a living out of coppicing oak for charcoal and making besom brooms, left in the 1960s. Holy Austin Rock may have been a medieval hermitage. Perched high on the hill above Kinver village, half-a-mile east of the fort, is the red sandstone church of St Peter dating from the fourteenth and fifteenth century.

Saint Chad, the first bishop of Lichfield, died during an outbreak of plague in AD 672 and was buried in St Mary's Church. Almost immediately, he was venerated as a saint, and in 700 his relics were enshrined in the first cathedral of Saint Peter. Shortly after, Bede recorded that in 'both places, as a testimony of his virtue, frequent miraculous cures are wont to be wrought.' He cites, for example, how a madman recovered his senses after spending the night near the bishop's grave. Drawn by such stories, pilgrims began to flock to Chad's shrine. Lichfield grew from a Saxon bishopric to a flourishing medieval town, with a weekly market and several annual fairs. Today – famed for its cathedral and literary associations – the city retains not only its market but a number of ancient customs, the oldest possibly dating back to pre-Roman times: the Shrovetide Fair, St George's Day Court, the Court of Arraye, Greenhill Bower and the Sheriff's Ride around the city boundaries.

But Lichfield is not alone in preserving its ancient traditions. Each of the seven Heart of England counties possesses a rich heritage of local customs, legends and folklore: the annual Horn Dance at Abbots Bromley, the ancient custom of collecting 'wroth silver' at Knightlow Cross, Ryton-on-Dunsmore, and the legendary ride of Lady Godiva through the streets of Coventry are but a few examples.

Although it may no longer be true today, in 1893 A. H. Walls wrote of Warwickshire, 'I have everywhere found amongst the lower classes a lingering belief in the existence of witches, ghosts, and devils.' It is not surprising, therefore, that tales of fairies, goblins, imps and other foul fiends flourished throughout the English heartland, as can be inferred from place names and from references in the works of Shakespeare and other local writers. Among the best-known locations for stories about the devil are Alcester, where the smiths grew devil's tails after refusing to stop work on Sundays; along the Wye Valley, in the exploits of Jack o'Kent, who sold his soul to the devil; and on the Stiperstones, where Satan himself is said to have presided over witches' gatherings. Monstrous creatures include the Montisford dragon, killed by the criminal Garson, and the hideous dun-cow of Dunsmore Heath, vanquished by Guy of Warwick.

On Kinver Edge in Staffordshire, early settlers carved houses out of the soft sandstone rock. Many of these curious dwellings were later fitted with doors, windows, fireplaces and chimneys, and embellished with stone, brick and tile. Although the last of the rock-dwellers left in the 1960s, the remoteness of the site has long been associated with mystery and legend. It is said, for example, that the caves were inhabited by two giants, one in Holy Austin Rock on Kinver Edge and the other in Samson's Cave at nearby Enville. They quarrelled and in a fit of rage the Kinver giant hurled a massive boulder at his neighbour. Known as the 'Bolt Stone', it is supposed to have landed in the Comptons to the south-west of Enville, but today the exact location of its whereabouts is unknown.

At Catthorpe in Warwickshire the Reverend Staresmore employed a novel, if untraditional, method of protecting his apples from scrumpers. In 1795 Samuel Ireland wrote: 'It was a custom with this whimsical being, at the latter end of the year, to tie a bull-dog to every apple-tree in his orchard, for the purpose of terrifying robbers.' A less anecdotal event took place on the Wrekin at dawn on Easter Sunday, at which time, it was maintained, the sun would dance. One woman, who could not believe that such an occurrence was possible, got up early and, according to an account of 1879, witnessed the sun dance three times. 'I used,' she said, 'not to believe it but now I can never doubt more.'

Another person who was to have doubts about his beliefs was Edward Wightman, a leading Protestant from Burton-upon-Trent who presented a petition to King James I strongly criticizing the Church of England. He was arrested and tried for heresy. On 11 April 1612, after being found guilty, he was taken to Lichfield market place and put to death – becoming the last person in England to be burnt at the stake. Thirty-nine years later, George Fox, founder of the Quaker movement, visited Lichfield and, claiming to hear the word of the Lord, cried: 'Woe to the bloody city of Lichfield.' He added: 'No one laid hands on me, but as I went thus crying through the streets there seemed to me to be a great channel of blood running down the streets, and the market place appeared like a pool of blood.' A grim reminder, perhaps, that – after the martyrdom of thousands of Christians at Lichfield by the Roman emperor Diocletian – the name of the city was long thought to mean 'field of corpses.'

Tamworth Castle
Tamworth

Almost 8 miles south-east of Lichfield, Tamworth Castle stands high on a steep artificial mound in the town centre, overlooking floral terraces, pleasure grounds and the confluence of the rivers Tame and Anker. A typical example of a Norman motte-and-bailey castle, it was first built towards the end of the eleventh century by Robert de Marmion, on part of the site of the fortress erected by Ethelfleda in 913 (a fortress which enclosed the entire Saxon town). The castle was rebuilt of sandstone during the twelfth century and all that remains of the early Norman fortification are stretches of herringbone walling. The Norman polygonal shell-keep has a square tower set into its walls on the east side. Over the centuries various owners have made numerous additions and alterations to the building, including the early fifteenth-century Banqueting Hall, the Tudor Warder's Lodge and the early seventeenth-century South Wing. The castle was purchased from the Marquess of Townshend by Tamworth Corporation in 1897 and opened to the public in 1899. It now houses the town's museum and contains a series of period room settings, dating from Norman times.

Lichfield House
Lichfield

Before the Norman Conquest, the ancient city of Lichfield was the ecclesiastical centre of the Anglo-Saxon kingdom of Mercia. It was recorded in the Domesday Book of 1086 as Licefelle or Lecefelle. The name was long thought to mean 'field of corpses', but modern interpretations favour 'grey forest'. Fourteen miles north-east of Birmingham, Lichfield is an important market centre serving the surrounding agricultural communities. Although its appearance is essentially Georgian, the basic layout of the streets is medieval. The timbered Lichfield House in Bore Street, dated 1510, is now a restaurant and confectioners. It stands next to the early eighteenth-century Donegal House (now an information centre) and the Guildhall (erected in 1846). Dr Samuel Johnson was born in a three-storeyed house in Breadmarket Street in 1709. It is now a museum and bookshop. Elias Ashmole, the antiquarian and astrologer who bequeathed his collection of antiquities and documents to Oxford University, was born nearby in 1617.

Lichfield Cathedral
Lichfield

The first cathedral church at Lichfield was consecrated in 700 to enshrine the bones of St Chad, the first bishop of Lichfield, who died in 672. A Norman stone cathedral was built on the site in 1135 at the instigation of Bishop Roger de Clinton. Dedicated to St Mary and St Chad, the present cathedral was built of red sandstone between 1195 and 1325. It is the only one in England with three spires, known as the 'Ladies of the Vale'. In the fourteenth century the Lady Chapel was added at the east end. The sixteenth-century glass in the chapel windows, brought to England in 1802, came originally from the Cistercian abbey at Herckenrode, near Liège in Belgium. During the Civil War the Parliamentarians demolished the central spire and severely damaged the rest of the cathedral. The building was restored during the reign of Charles II, but much rebuilding was again necessary in the late eighteenth century because of decay. Housed within the thirteenth-century Chapter House is the priceless Lichfield Gospels, an illuminated manuscript dating from the early eighth century.

Letocetum
Wall

The Romano-British settlement at Wall, just over two miles south of Lichfield, was situated on the Roman road of Watling Street – the principal route to North Wales and Ireland up until the coming of the railways in the mid-nineteenth century. The name 'Letocetum' is derived from the Celtic 'Leitocaiton', meaning 'grey wood'. Evidence suggests that the settlement was also a small legionary fortress. Research indicates that the town buildings covered an area of between 20 and 30 acres. Most of the stone, however, was removed for use as building material in Lichfield and Shenstone. The remains at Wall include parts of the bath-house, comprising a furnace, hypocaust (now filled in to prevent frost damage) and cold, warm and hot baths, and the stone foundations of what is possibly a hostel or 'Mansio', where messengers on the imperial route could rest overnight and change horses. The latter is thought to have been destroyed by fire in about AD 160–70. The site is managed by English Heritage and contains a small museum. The church of St John in the nearby village of Wall was designed by Scott and Moffatt and consecrated in 1843.

Moseley Old Hall
near Wolverhampton

After his defeat at the battle of Worcester in 1651 Charles II fled north to White Ladies and Boscobel House. Leaving Boscobel on the night of 7 September, disguised as a woodcutter, he arrived, early the following morning, at Moseley Hall (later Moseley Old Hall) and was met by Thomas Whitegreave and Father Huddlestone. Whitegreave later admitted: 'When he came to the door with the Penderels guarding him, he was so habited like one of them that I could not tell which was he, only I knew all the rest.' The king stayed two days at Moseley before setting off for Bentley Hall, about 4 miles south-east, leaving there on 10 September in the guise of William Jackson, servant of Mrs Jane Lane. Moseley Hall at that time was situated in a remote part of the Staffordshire countryside, surrounded by its own agricultural estate. It now lies on the northern fringe of Wolverhampton, about 4 miles north of the city centre. The house, with its secret hideouts, is Elizabethan but was altered in about 1870 when the Elizabethan windows were replaced by casements and the outer walls covered in brick. It was acquired by the National Trust in 1962.

Essex Bridge
Great Haywood

The 'No-Through Road', leading from the village of Great Haywood to Shugborough, crosses the River Trent by way of a fourteen-arched bridge, some 4 feet wide and about 100 feet long, reputed to be the longest packhorse bridge in England. The 1st Earl of Essex, after whom it is named, is thought to have erected the bridge in the latter half of the sixteenth century. Built of stone, with a series of cutwaters on both sides, it replaced an earlier wooden bridge. An eighteenth-century engraving, after a watercolour by Moses Griffith, inaccurately depicts the bridge as having at least twenty-two arches. Suitable only for pedestrians, Essex Bridge is sited near the confluence of the rivers Trent, Sow and Sow (New Cut). Running alongside the Trent at Shugborough is the Trent and Mersey Canal, which joins the Staffordshire and Worcestershire Canal at Great Haywood Junction. The railway line between Rugeley and Stafford crosses the southern part of Shugborough Park by means of a bridge and tunnel, constructed in 1847. Designed by John Livock, one of the tunnel entrances is in Egyptian style, while the other is mock-medieval with turrets and battlements.

The West Front
Shugborough

Shugborough, the ancestral home of the Earls of Lichfield, lies on the northern edge of Cannock Chase, midway between Rugeley and Stafford. The estate was purchased in 1624, by William Anson, whose great grandsons, Thomas (1695–1773) and George (1696–1762), were responsible for enlarging the mansion, landscaping the park and commissioning the unique collection of neo-classical monuments. George became the First Lord of the Admiralty in 1747 and, having made his fortune from an epic four-year circumnavigation of the globe, he financed his elder brother's plans to transform the family estate at Shugborough. In the process the medieval village in front of the house was demolished and the inhabitants re-settled at Great Haywood. The Mansion House, originally built in 1693 by their father William, was extended between 1745 and 1748, and was further enlarged by Samuel Wyatt between 1790 and 1806. The house and surrounding parkland was given to the National Trust after the 4th Earl's death in 1960 but is now managed and maintained by Staffordshire County Council. Part of the house continues to be lived in by the 5th Earl, Patrick Lichfield.

Stafford Castle
Stafford

In 1070, on a site near the North Gate of Stafford, beside the River Sow, William the Conqueror ordered the construction of a castle. It was probably erected within the defences of the old Saxon town, fortified by Ethelfleda in 913. By 1086, however, it had been demolished. A second castle (of the motte-and-bailey type) was built on a high undulating ridge, one mile west of the town centre, probably by Robert de Toeni (Robert of Stafford) at the end of the eleventh century. It was rebuilt by Ralph de Stafford, 1st Earl of Stafford, in the mid-fourteenth century and consisted of a rectangular stone keep (120 feet by 50 feet) with octagonal towers at each corner. A thriving settlement or 'vill of the castle' grew up around the site, but by 1467 it had been abandoned and the houses totally destroyed. In July 1643, after the Royalist garrison had fled, the castle was occupied by the Parliamentarians and soon after it was ordered to be demolished. Reconstruction in the Gothic Revival style began in 1813 by Sir George Jerningham, later Lord Stafford. The deteriorated remains of the incomplete rebuilding were acquired by Stafford Borough Council in 1961.

Biddulph Grange
Biddulph

Enter the 15-acre garden of Biddulph Grange and you step not only into the past, but into one of the most unusual and surprising gardens in England. Created between 1846 and 1871, it was conceived and constructed by James Bateman, a wealthy industrialist, and his wife Maria. Their friend Edward Cooke, the marine artist, gave them specialist help and assistance. Bateman, who was also a horticulturist and plant collector, divided the overall garden into a number of smaller gardens designed to accommodate some of the rare and exotic plants he (or others) had gathered from various parts of the world. Biddulph was bought by Robert Heath in 1871. The house was largely destroyed by fire in 1896 and subsequently rebuilt. It was converted into a hospital in 1923 and from the 1960s the gardens suffered increasingly from vandalism and neglect. Biddulph Grange was bought by the National Trust in 1988. After a painstaking restoration programme, it was opened to the public on 1 May 1991 and is a rare example of a high Victorian garden. Among its exciting attractions are The Cheshire Cottage, Egypt, The Italian Garden, China, The Glen, The Stumpery, and The Dahlia Walk.

Shrewsbury and Shropshire

Severn Valley from Leighton

On elevated ground between the wooded slopes of the Wrekin and the green meadows of the River Severn, Leighton is said to be the most beautifully situated village in Shropshire. The parish church of St Mary the Virgin was rebuilt in 1714, using much of the masonry of the earlier medieval church. Inside are a number of monuments dedicated to members of the Leighton and Kynnersley families. Attached to the rear of the Kynnersley Arms is the old mill building, with the mill-wheel still in evidence. Iron ore was smelted in the village from at least the sixteenth century, using coal, mined locally. During the Industrial Revolution the furnaces were used by Abraham Darby. Leighton Hall, built in 1778, stands in the meadows to the south of the village, overlooking the river, with views to Wenlock Edge and the Stretton Hills. In the grounds is Leighton Lodge, the birthplace of the novelist Mary Webb (1881–1927). The village is some 9 miles south-east of Shrewsbury.

In their classic work *A History of Shrewsbury* (1825) Owen and Blakeway quote the following description of the town:

Oliver Mathews, who in the reign of James I amused his age with penning 'An Account of the situation, foundation, and ancient names of the famous Town of Salop, not inferior to many Cities in this Realm for antiquity, goodly government, good orders and wealth,' delivers himself in the following terms. 'This most ancient and famous town was Moell-mynd, whom the Romans, Saxons, Normans and Danes, called Mulmutius Dunwallo. The which foundation was first begun about 669 years after Brutus' first entrance into Britain, which before was called Albion, anno mundi 3525, before the incarnation of our Saviour Christ 438. This most noble king, Dyffenwall Moell-mynd, made the Castle there, and the North Gate, and a wall from the Castle to Severn, and also from the Castle to the Severn on the north side; leaving Severn to be a wall and a defence to the town round abouts, saving the wall before mentioned: and called the town by her first name, *Caer Odder yn Hafren*, which is by interpretation, "The City or the Town of falling or sliding ground within the womb of Severn"'.

Owen and Blakeway, however, argued that although a Welsh prince named Dyffenwall did exist and Shrewsbury may have owed its foundation to the Celtic Britons, the town was built 'after the Saxon invasion'.

Although Shrewsbury was located only 5 miles north-west of the Roman city of Viroconium (Wroxeter), no evidence of Roman occupation has been found in the town. During the sixth century AD, the settlement was known by its Welsh name of Pengwern, meaning 'hill of alders'. It is reputed that Brocwael, King of Powys, had a palace on the hill where the remains of old St Chad's church now stands. By the ninth century the town was part of the kingdom of Mercia (which encompassed all of the Heart of England) and was known by the Anglo-Saxon name of Scrobbesbyrig, thought to mean the 'town on the shrub-covered hill'.

Towards the end of the ninth century King Alfred the Great granted Mercia to his son-in-law, Ethelred. After Ethelred's death in 911 his widow and Alfred's eldest daughter, Ethelfleda, became the ruler of the kingdom. During one of her frequent visits to Shrewsbury she founded the church dedicated to St Alkmund. By the mid-tenth century Shrewsbury was an important administrative centre in the Severn valley and one of a select number of towns or cities allowed by law to mint coins.

Because of the town's close proximity to Wales, it was often subject to border hostilities (the border, however, was not fixed; it ebbed and flowed like the tide, depending which side, English or Welsh, had gained or lost territory). Shrewsbury, ideally sited for defensive purposes, stood on a hill, within a tight loop of the Severn, with a narrow neck of land providing the only dry-shod approach to the town. During Saxon rule this was guarded by a timber fortification, sited where the castle now stands. According to the Domesday Book Shrewsbury contained 252 houses and had a population of nearly one thousand. Within the town walls there were four principal churches: St Alkmund's, St Chad's, St Julian's and St Mary's.

After the Norman Conquest William allowed Earl Edwin of Mercia to retain his Mercian kingdom. Edwin was killed during an Anglo-Saxon rebellion led by Edric Syvaticus, or Edric the Wild, and the earldom of Shrewsbury was conferred on Roger de Montgomery, a kinsman of the Conqueror. On the site of the old wooden church of St Peter, which stood outside the loop of the river, he founded the Benedictine abbey of St Peter and St Paul in 1083. Before his death in 1094 Roger enlarged and strengthened the castle at Shrewsbury and from this stronghold led several campaigns across the border into Wales. During the summer of 1138 the Norman castle, built of red sandstone, was besieged and taken by King Stephen. Apart from the gateway very little of the Norman building survives, much of it having been demolished during Edward I's rebuilding of the fortress in about 1300.

Before and after Edward's conquest of Wales in 1283, Shropshire and the borderlands suffered from innumerable local skirmishes and several major wars. These included the battles between King John and Llywelyn the Great, which continued well into the reign of Henry III (1216–72), and the battles of Shrewsbury (1403) and Mortimer's Cross (1461), fought during the Wars of the Roses. The Civil War affected the whole of the region, but the major battles occurred east of the River Severn at Edge Hill (1642), Cropredy Bridge (1644), Naseby (1645) and Worcester (1651). By whatever name – Pengwern, Scrobbesbyrig, Salop or Shrewsbury – the county town of Shropshire not only treasures its special place in English history, but shares it proudly with the Welsh.

Heath Chapel
near Clee St Margaret

All that remains of the medieval village of Heath, apart from extensive earthworks, is a small and simple chapel built of sandstone by the Normans over 800 years ago. It is considered to be one of the most perfect examples of its kind in England. Except for the addition of a tiny nineteenth-century window, it has survived unaltered. Inside, most of the furniture is seventeenth century. While, on the south wall of the nave, there are traces of a fresco thought to depict St George and the Dragon. Eyton noted in 1857: 'Of its history I can learn nothing, and only judge by analogy that it was founded by some Layman, holding the Manor of the Prior of Wenlock in the twelfth century. Its parochial subjection to the Church of Stoke St Milburg [sic] is undoubted. In such a case we should not expect any evidence as to its endowment or Incumbents. The Monastic appropriation of the Mother Church had the usual effect on the Daughter, whose existence during four centuries is unrecorded, and whose Altar, for much of that period, was probably unserved.' If the chapel was ever dedicated to a saint, the name has been long forgotten. It is still used regularly for services.

Whittington Castle
Whittington

Two miles north-east of Oswestry in the large village of Whittington are the ruins of a medieval grey-stone castle, with a wide water-filled moat and thirteenth-century gatehouse. The earliest-known fortress on the site was built in 845 by a Welsh chieftain. It was once surrounded and protected by marshland, but this has now been drained. Shortly after the Norman Conquest the castle was rebuilt, probably by Roger de Montgomery. Although the estate passed to his eldest son Roger de Bellême, it was confiscated in 1102 by Henry I. Shortly after, the manor was granted to the Peverel family. Henry II gave it briefly to Geoffrey de Vere in 1164, but the following year granted it to Roger de Powys. Fulk Fitz Warin, who owned the manor at the beginning of the thirteenth century, rebuilt and enlarged the Norman fortress. Sited close to the border, it was attacked by the Welsh on several occasions and was reputedly captured by Llywelyn the Great in 1223. By the late eighteenth century the castle was a ruin, much of its stone having been used for road repairs.

Old Oswestry Hill Fort
Oswestry

Located to the north of the old market town of Oswestry are the extensive earthwork remains of an Iron Age hill-fort, covering around 40 acres. It is thought to date from around the fifth century BC, but was abandoned after the Roman conquest. It may, however, have been briefly reoccupied during the Dark Ages and perhaps again during the Middle Ages. Anderson observes in *Shropshire: its Early History and Antiquities* (1864): 'Fortifications of British origin generally have but a couple of ditches drawn round the quarter most liable to attack; in the extraordinary fortress of Hen Dinas, at Old Oswestry, however, there are four or five concentric ditches.' Oswestry is named after St Oswald, King of Northumbria, who was killed at the battle of Maserfield (thought to be Oswestry) in AD 642. The large parish church, dating from Norman times, is dedicated to the saint. Damaged during the Civil War, it was largely rebuilt in 1675 and restored in 1874, 1955 and 1977. The high mound in the centre of the town, near Horsemarket, is all that remains of the Norman castle, built by Reginald the Sheriff prior to 1086.

Offa's Dyke
near Carreg-y-Big

To mark the boundary between England and Wales, in the latter half of the eighth century, Offa, King of Mercia, ordered the construction of a massive earthwork mound and ditch, stretching, with some gaps, from the River Severn, near Chepstow, in the south to the mouth of the River Dee, near Prestatyn, in the north. Although the boundary covered a distance of about 150 miles, Offa's Dyke accounted for only 80 miles of the total. It is thought to have originally been some 60 feet high, with a ditch 12 feet deep on the Welsh side. Despite the passage of time, significant stretches of the dyke can still be traced, notably in the area around Rhydycroesau and Carreg-y-Big, a few miles west of Oswestry. In 1971 Offa's Dyke Path, a 176-mile-long footpath, was opened, following about 60 miles of the best-preserved stretches of the ancient earthwork. To the east of the dyke, extending from the Dee estuary, near Flint, in the north to Maesbury, near Oswestry, in the south, are traces of an earlier and shorter earthwork known as Wat's Dyke.

St Peter's Church
Melverley

One of the very few timber-framed churches in the county, St Peter's stands on the site of an earlier church which was burned down by the Welsh under Owain Glyndwr (or Glendower) in 1401. The present church was constructed shortly after of local timber, wattle and daub. It was restored in the early eighteenth century, with further restorations in 1878, 1924 and 1991. The village of Melverley borders Wales and lies on the east bank of the River Vyrnwy, some 10 miles west of Shrewsbury. It is thought that there was a small hermitage on the river bank in late Saxon times. At the time of the Norman survey of 1086 the manor was held by Rainault, kinsman of William I and deputy to Roger de Montgomery, Earl of Shrewsbury. The parish was part of the Welsh diocese of St Asaph until the 1920s when it was transferred to the English diocese of Lichfield. In the churchyard a tombstone to John Parry, who died on 17 August 1858, aged twenty-one, reads:

All you young men that pass me by,
As you are now so once was I,
As I am now, so you must be,
Therefore prepare to follow me.

Haughmond Abbey
Haughmond

Sheltering beneath the wooded north-western slopes of Haughmond Hill, 3 miles north-east of Shrewsbury, are the extensive ruins of Haughmond Abbey, founded by William FitzAlan in about 1135 for Augustinian canons. After its dissolution in 1539, the abbey church and many of the monastic buildings were demolished. All that now remains of the twelfth-century church, apart from the foundations, is the doorway leading to the western range of the cloister. The chapter house, with its three magnificent carved arches (the middle one being the main doorway), dates from the late twelfth century. Most of the buildings which were not destroyed, including the abbot's lodging, the great hall and the kitchens, were incorporated into a private house by the Littleton family. It was burnt down during the Civil War. The abbey is now in the care of English Heritage. The photograph depicts the view across the remains of the abbot's private chamber to the infirmary hall. On the summits of Haughmond Hill and nearby Ebury Hill are the earthwork remains of Iron Age hill-forts.

Haughmond Hill
from Uffington

On the summit of the wooded Haughmond Hill, 3 miles north-east of Shrewsbury, are the remains of an Iron Age hill-fort and an earthwork called Queen Eleanor's Bower. The hill is also scarred with old, disused quarry workings, the rock having been used for roadstone. To the west, on the east bank of the Severn, is the ancient village of Uffington. The church was rebuilt in 1856 by S. P. Smith, while the windows contain Flemish and German glass dating from the sixteenth and seventeenth centuries. During the late eighteenth and early nineteenth centuries, when the upper Severn was navigable, Uffington was a river port, like Shrewsbury, Montford and Pool Quay, near Welshpool. For many years there was a ferry across the Severn, operating between the village and Monkmoor fields. The name Uffington means 'the settlement of Uffa's people'. About a mile north of the village is the site of Sundorne Castle, a castellated brick mansion rebuilt in the early nineteenth century and demolished in 1956. All that now survives are the remains of the gatehouse and chapel.

English Bridge
Shrewsbury

This regional capital – variously known as Pengwern, Scrobbesbyrig, Salop, and Shrewsbury – lies on a rocky hill within a tight loop of the River Severn, just 9 miles or so east of the Welsh border. In about 1540 Leland wrote: 'There be two great main bridges of stone on the whole river of Severn at Scrobbesbyrig. The greatest and fairest and highest upon the stream is the Welsh Bridge having six great arches of stone, so called because it is the way out of the town into Wales. This bridge standeth on the west side of the town, and hath at the one end of it a great gate to enter by into the town, and at the other end toward Wales a mighty strong tower to prohibit enemies to enter onto the bridge. The second bridge is lower on Severn . . . and this hath four great arches beside the drawbridge.' The latter bridge, known as the East or Stone or English Bridge, had houses upon it and stood near the Benedictine Abbey of St Peter and St Paul. Both bridges were later replaced: the Welsh Bridge by one with five arches in 1795 and the English Bridge by one with seven arches in 1774.

The Quarry
Shrewsbury

Below the remains of the medieval town walls and the new church of St Chad lies 29 acres of public parkland, known as The Quarry, first laid out in 1719. The quarry itself was converted in 1879 into the Dingle, which now forms the centrepiece of the park, with spectacular floral displays, a small lake and the Shoemaker's Arbour, dated 1679 and re-erected by the lake in 1879. The statue of Sabrina, Goddess of the River Severn, is by Peter Hollins. During heavy flooding the park is often submerged. On the hill overlooking the park is the new church of St Chad, designed by George Steuart on an unusual circular plan and built by John Simpson in 1790–92. The old church of St Chad stands much further east, near the junction of Belmont, Princess Street and Milk Street. It collapsed in 1788 and was demolished, except for the Lady Chapel. In addition to St Chad's, the parish churches of St Alkmund's, St Julian's and St Mary's all stood within the town walls.

Attingham Park
Attingham

Straddling the River Tern, some 4 miles south-east of Shrewsbury, Attingham Park covers 3,826 acres, part of which occupies the site of the Roman city of Viroconium. Built of Grinshill stone for Noel Hill, 1st Lord Berwick, by George Steuart between 1783 and 1785, Attingham Hall incorporates parts of an early eighteenth-century house called Tern Hall. The wooded park was landscaped by Humphrey Repton in 1797 and is stocked with fallow deer. The property, including the house, the park and thirteen farms, was bequeathed to the National Trust by the 8th Lord Berwick, who died in 1947. At the south-west corner of the park, near a ford of the River Severn, is the village of Atcham (its name is derived from Attingham, signifying 'the home of Eata's people'). The old village was essentially destroyed when the grounds of Attingham Park were extended and landscaped in the eighteenth century. The Old Malt House was given to the village by Lord Berwick in 1926. The early thirteenth-century tower of the church of St Eata was probably partly built with stones from Viroconium. Born in the village in 1075, the historian Ordericus Vitalis was baptized in the church.

Roman City
Wroxeter

The ruins of ancient Viroconium, the fourth largest city in Roman Britain, lie to the north of the village and church of Wroxeter, 5 miles south-east of Shrewsbury. Excavations have established that it was founded in the first century AD as a legionary fortress. There is no evidence, however, to suggest that the Celtic-British tribe of the Cornovii ever settled here, despite the fact that they occupied the Iron Age hill-fort on the summit of the nearby Wrekin. It was from this and other fortresses, situated on the main supply route of Watling Street, that the Romans launched campaigns across the Shropshire border and into Wales. The shattered pieces of a 12-foot-long and 4-foot-high stone inscription were discovered in the 1920s. It originally stood above the entrance of the forum and, when reconstructed, stated in Latin that the building was erected by the Community of the Cornovii in honour of the Emperor Hadrian in AD 130. Viroconium is in the care of English Heritage and contains a small museum.

River Severn and Berrington
from Atcham

Having made a tight loop around Shrewsbury, the River Severn wriggles and turns for some 9 miles before it reaches the village of Atcham, with its two bridges: the old bridge, built of stone in 1769–71 by John Gwynne, and the new bridge, built of concrete by Salop County Council and opened in 1929. About a mile across the fields on the other side of the river is a distinctive house with a round tower, called Cronkhill. It was designed by John Nash and is said to be the earliest Italianate villa ever built in England. It is almost certainly the 'Villa in Shropshire' exhibited at the Royal Academy in 1802. The red sandstone church of All Saints in the village of Berrington stands on Saxon foundations. It contains the fourteenth-century oak effigy of a cross-legged knight, reputed to have been killed by the boar which lies at his feet. The timber-framed manor house opposite the church is dated 1658. The photograph depicts the view south-west from Atcham across the Severn, past Cronkhill house and Berrington church, to Caer Caradoc and the Stretton Hills.

Chamomile Field
near the Wrekin

Rising in lonely isolation from the level fields and rich farmland of the broad Shropshire plain is the Wrekin, the summit of which is 1,335 feet above sea-level. During the Iron Age the volcanic hog-back hill was the site of a fort built by the ancient Britons, and may have been the administrative capital of the Cornovii tribe, whose territory covered much of Shropshire just prior to the Roman conquest. Leland wrote in about 1540: 'The Wrekin hill, of some called Mount Gilbert. The roots of this hill standing by the left rype [sic] of Severn be not past a mile from Wroxeter. This Wrekin hill is the highest ground of all the country thereabout, and standeth as a Pharos, barren of wood. There is in the top of this hill a delicate plain ground bearing good fine grass, and in this plain is a fair fountain.' A beacon fire was lit on the hill in 1588 to warn of the sighting of the Spanish Armada. The Wrekin is rich in legends and folklore. The mounds in the photograph should not be mistaken for the hill.

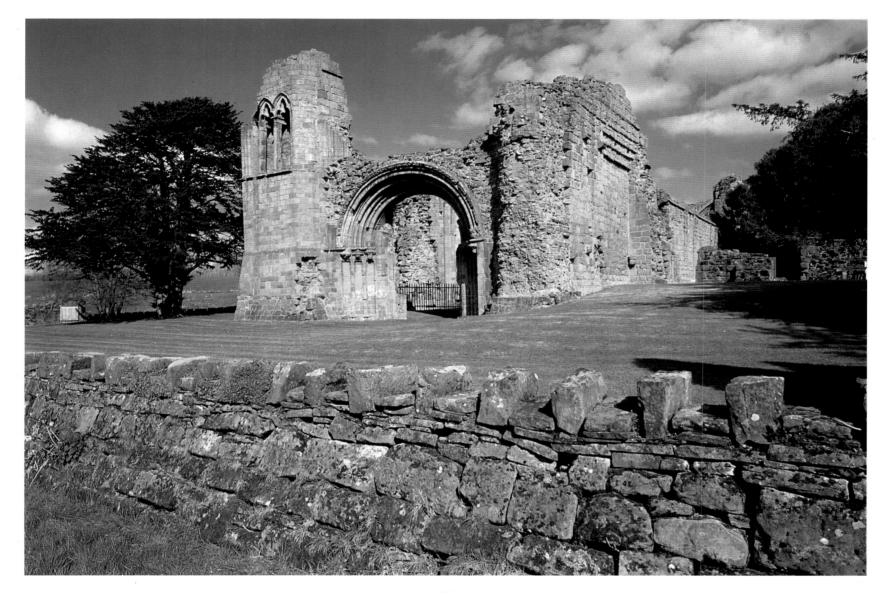

Lilleshall Abbey
Lilleshall

Amidst the fields one mile south of the village of Lilleshall are the ruins of an Augustinian abbey founded in about 1148 by Richard de Belmeis as a monastery of the Arrouasian order. It consisted of a small community of Arrouasian canons from Tong, near Shifnal, which had originally been brought to Shropshire from Dorchester in Oxfordshire by Belmeis's brother Philip. This order (taking its name from Arrouaise in France) was later absorbed by the Augustinians. After Lilleshall Abbey was dissolved in 1538 the lands were granted to William Cavendish, ancestor of the Dukes of Devonshire. One year later he sold them to James Leveson of Wolverhampton. During the Civil War the abbey was converted into a Royalist stronghold and, in consequence, those buildings which managed to survive the Dissolution were badly damaged by the Parliamentarians. The 70-foot-high obelisk on Lilla's Hill was erected in 1839 in memory of George Granville Leveson-Gower, 1st Duke of Sutherland, who died in 1833. His residence, Lilleshall Hall, was built in 1829 by Sir Jeffry Wyatville and is now a national sports centre.

Boscobel House
near Brewood

On 3 September 1651 Charles II and his Royalist forces were defeated by the Parliamentarians at the Battle of Worcester. The king fled north with his followers, and by dawn the following day they had reached White Ladies, owned by Frances Cotton. Shortly after, disguised as a countryman, Charles left the house on foot with Richard Penderel of nearby Hubbal Grange and spent the day sheltering in Spring Coppice wood. That night the two men set off for Madeley, intending to cross the Severn into Wales. The Severn crossings were closely guarded, however, and they were forced to retrace their steps. Just before daybreak on 6 September they arrived at Boscobel House (also owned by Cotton), where Charles found one of his officers, Major William Careless, in hiding. That day Careless and the king hid in the branches of a nearby oak tree. Charles left Boscobel the next day and on 16 October reached safety in France. Boscobel House was built by the Giffards in about 1630 as a hunting lodge. In the grounds is the Royal Oak, a successor to the one hidden in by Charles. Boscobel and White Ladies Priory are owned by English Heritage.

Severn Gorge
Ironbridge

Spanning the heavily wooded limestone cliffs of the narrow Severn Gorge at Ironbridge, 12 miles south-east of Shrewsbury, is the world's first cast-iron bridge. Designed by Thomas Farnolls Pritchard, a Shrewsbury joiner by profession, the Iron Bridge was cast by Abraham Darby III's Coalbrookdale Company and erected in 1779. It was opened on New Year's Day 1781. Since 1936 its use has been restricted to that of a footbridge. The Tollhouse at the southern end of the bridge houses an exhibition about the bridge. A proposal by Shropshire County Council to build a three-span, steel-frame concrete bridge close to Darby's world-famous single-arched span was defeated at a public enquiry in 1990. The town of Ironbridge, running along the north bank of the gorge, takes its name from the bridge and dates essentially from the late eighteenth century. The Market House, with five segmental arches on the ground floor, originally open, dates from about 1790. The church of St Luke, designed by Thomas Smith of Madeley, was built in 1836. On the banks of the Severn, in the shadow of the bridge, traditional Severn coracles are still made.

China Museum
Coalport

The 4-mile stretch of the Severn, between Coalport and Coalbrookdale, has been heralded as the birthplace of the Industrial Revolution. It became Britain's first declared World Heritage site in late 1986. In addition to the Iron Bridge and Tollhouse there are six main museums: the Coalport China Museum, where china was made until 1926, when the company moved to Staffordshire; the Museum of Iron and the Darby Furnace, illustrating the history of ironmaking and the story of the Coalbrookdale Company; the Museum of the River and Visitor Centre, housed in the Severn Warehouse, which was built in the 1840s, and offering an introduction to the history of the Severn Gorge; the Jackfield Tile Museum, exhibiting locally made decorative wall and floor tiles from the 1850s to the 1960s and showing live tile manufacture; Rosehill House, a restored ironmaster's home of the early nineteenth century; and Blists Hill Open Air Museum, a 50-acre site in which the visitor can enter the gas-lit streets of a working industrial Victorian town. Among smaller sites are the Tar Tunnel, originally cut in 1786, and Bedlam Furnaces, built in 1757.

Buildwas Abbey
Buildwas

Buildwas Abbey, on the opposite bank of the River Severn to the village of Buildwas, was founded in 1135 by Roger de Clinton, Bishop of Lichfield and Coventry, for Savigniac monks. Dedicated to Our Lady and St Chad, the house became Cistercian in 1147, when the Savigniac and Cistercian orders were united: a union confirmed at the Council of Reims in March the following year. Thereafter, the grey habits of Savigny were replaced by the white habits of Cîteaux. The abbey was surrendered to Henry VIII in 1536 and subsequently demolished. The extensive remains are impressive, with the church surviving almost intact except for the roofs and the outer walls of the aisles and the chapel. The remains are reputed to be haunted by the ghost of the abbot who was murdered in 1342. Dating from 1720, the church of Holy Trinity in Buildwas village was largely constructed with Grinshill stone taken from the abbey ruins. The name Buildwas is thought to be derived from the Old English *byld* and *waesse*, meaning 'the building in a marshy place'.

Bridgnorth Castle
Bridgnorth

Located within the grounds of a public park, on the summit of a high ridge overlooking the River Severn, are the sparse remains of Bridgnorth Castle, built by Roger de Bellême, son of Roger de Montgomery, in about 1100. Shortly after, Bellême conspired with others to dethrone Henry I and place the English crown on the head of Robert of Normandy, the king's elder brother. In 1102, after a three-month siege, Henry captured the castle and Bellême, who surrendered at Shrewsbury, was exiled and his estates forfeited to the Crown. By the close of the thirteenth century the fortress had declined in importance and was allowed to fall into decay. All that remains today is part of the keep, which leans at a seemingly perilous angle of seventeen degrees from the perpendicular. The old market town of Bridgnorth, with numerous timber-framed buildings, is divided into Low Town and High Town by the red sandstone ridge. Near the Severn Valley steam railway station is a large mound known as Panpudding Hill, the site of an ancient fortification.

Acton Burnell Castle
Acton Burnell

Acton Burnell castle was built of red sandstone towards the end of the thirteenth century by Robert Burnell, Bishop of Bath and Wells and Lord Chancellor under Edward I. Although called a castle, it is more accurately a fortified manor house, crenellated in 1284. It was probably abandoned in the latter half of the fifteenth century. The manor was acquired by the Smythes in the seventeenth century, and in 1934 their descendants placed the ruins in the care of English Heritage. The two stone gables near the castle are believed to be the remains of a great barn, 157 feet long and 40 feet wide. Here, it is claimed, Edward I summoned the first full English Parliament in 1283. The church of St Mary, close by, dates from the thirteenth century and contains monuments to the Lee family, ancestors of General Robert E. Lee, a Confederate leader in the American Civil War. Acton Burnell Hall, formerly the home of the Smythe family, became a convent of the Sisters of the Order of Sion in 1939. It is now a college of further education, known as Concord College.

Caer Caradoc and the Lawley
from Acton Burnell

Like the Wrekin and Earl's Hill, near Pontesbury, the underlying rock of Caer Caradoc Hill (1,506 feet) and the Lawley (1,236 feet) is volcanic, formed some 900 million years ago from molten lava and ash. Running parallel to the east of the Stretton Hills, of which Caer Caradoc and the Lawley are a part, is the pale limestone escarpment of Wenlock Edge, while to the west is the warm sandstone plateau of the Long Mynd. Caer Caradoc is named after Caradoc, or Caratacus, the British chieftain who stubbornly resisted the might of the conquering Roman legions until his defeat and capture in AD 51. Legend says that he made his heroic last stand from the Iron Age hill-fort on its rocky summit (the actual site described by Cornelius Tacitus, the Roman historian, is unknown). On the western slopes of the hill is a small cavern, popularly known as 'Caratacus's Cave'. The Lawley also has the earthwork remains of a prehistoric hill-fort on its summit. In the gap between the two hills lies the hamlet of Comley.

Mitchell's Fold
Stapeley Hill

Erected over 3,500 years ago by the people of the Bronze Age, Mitchell's Fold Stone Circle stands on Stapeley Hill, some 2 miles east of Chirbury. Around 80 feet in diameter and elliptical in shape, the ancient ring contains only fifteen stones out of what is thought to have originally been thirty-seven. The tallest is six feet high. Although its purpose remains a mystery, it is thought to have had some religious or ceremonial function. Among the numerous legends connected with the stones is the story of an old witch called Mitchell, who was turned into stone by a fairy after she had milked the magical cow of Stapeley Hill dry. The cow appeared in the circle each day to provide the local inhabitants with an everlasting supply of milk. The witch, however, tricked the cow into yielding all its milk by using a sieve. The cow collapsed exhausted and vanished, never to appear again. The tallest stone is said to be the witch, while the rest were erected to prevent her from escaping.

Stiperstones
near Pennerley

At 1,762 feet above sea-level, the Stiperstones are the second-highest range of hills in Shropshire. Situated 12 miles south-west of Shrewsbury, the long dark ridge is formed of hard white quartzite, which was shattered into regular block-like patterns by frost action during the last Ice Age. The Stiperstones were purchased by the Nature Conservancy Council in 1981 and the following year the area was declared a National Nature Reserve. Apart from the jagged, rubble-strewn ridge of quartzite tors, most of the 1,015-acre reserve is heathland, covered with gorse, heather and bilberries (known locally as wimberries). Among the numerous legends associated with the area, several affirm that it was the haunt of witches. The highest of the jagged tors along the ridge is known as the Devil's Chair; it is here that the Devil is said to have sat while presiding over the witches' gatherings. Edric Syvaticus, or Edric the Wild, is also reputed to haunt the hills. He led an unsuccessful Anglo-Welsh rebellion against the invading Normans.

Church Stretton
from Carding Mill Valley

The small market town of Church Stretton lies in the heart of Stretton Dale, between the volcanic ridge of the Stretton Hills and the wild moorland plateau of the Long Mynd. Over the north door of the Norman church of St Lawrence is an ancient fertility figure, known as a 'Sheela-na-gig'. Church Stretton became a fashionable health resort and spa town after the arrival of the railway in the late nineteenth century. Many of its half-timbered buildings, including 'Woodcote' (hidden by trees above the old cemetery), date from late Victorian or Edwardian times. Tudor Cottage, near the United Reform Church in High Street, was built shortly after the great fire of 1593. The town is a natural starting point for walks or excursions into the surrounding hills. The deep valleys which run south-east into Stretton Dale are known locally as batches or hollows. Between Townbrook Hollow and The Batch is the Carding Mill Valley, the most popular of the valleys, at the steep head of which is the Lightspout Waterfall. Most of the unenclosed land north of Milton Batch on the Long Mynd is owned by the National Trust.

All Saints' Church
Little Stretton

Around 2 miles south-west of Church Stretton, the village of Little Stretton lies in the narrowing valley of Stretton Dale between the towering bulks of the Long Mynd and Ragleth Hill. The timber-framed church of All Saints, with its thatched roof and wooden bell turret, was built as a chapel of ease in 1903 by Alice Elizabeth Gibbon, who died in 1932. She lived at the Manor House nearby, which – although much restored – dates from about 1600, with an eighteenth-century doorway and pediment. The timber- and stone-built Tan House, with its thatched porch and tiled roof, was the home of Derwent Wood (who paid for the thatched church roof). Pevsner says that it was 'flamboyantly restored and enriched when Derwent Wood lived there.' The timber box-framed Malt House, opposite, dates from about 1500 with seventeenth-century additions. The large barn with its unusual vertical weather-boarding (mentioned by Pevsner) has been demolished. Just north of the village, on the wooded slopes of the Long Mynd, stand the ruins of Brockhurst (or Brocards) Castle, thought to have been built by Henry II in about 1155. It was probably destroyed in the early thirteenth century.

Clee Hill and Teme Valley
from Clee Hill

The highest of the hills in Shropshire are the Clee Hills, some 5 miles east of Ludlow, comprising Clee Hill (approximately 1,540 feet), Titterstone Clee (1,749 feet) and Brown Clee (1,772 feet). The rocks of these comparatively young hills (less than 400 million years old) are formed of Old Red Sandstone, capped with a hard protective layer of volcanic rock known locally as 'dhustone' (also the name of a nearby village). On the summits of each of the hills, heavily scarred by abandoned mining and quarry workings, are numerous prehistoric sites. The hills were described by Michael Drayton in his topographical poem *Poly-Olbion* (1612–22):

Those Mountains of command
(the Clees, like loving twins, and
 Titterstone that stand)
Trans-severed, behold fair
 England towards the rise,
And on their setting side, how
 ancient Cambria lies.

The view south from the village of Clee Hill embraces the lower slopes of Clee Hill and the fertile valley of the River Teme with its green fields, woodland pockets and scattered farmsteads.

St Milburgha's Church
Stoke St Milborough

Nestling in a deep valley on the south-eastern slopes of Brown Clee, the village of Stoke St Milborough is noted for its associations with St Milburga, the first abbess of Wenlock Priory, who died in 715. Legend says that while being pursued by bloodhounds on the Clee Hills, the saint fell exhausted from her horse and at the exact spot where she landed a spring burst forth. Refreshed by the miraculous water, she was able to escape. The spring, known as St Milburga's Well, became a small centre for pilgrimage and the settlement that grew up around it became known as God's Stoke, recorded in the Domesday Book as 'Godestoch'. St Milburgha's (*sic*) Church, built in the thirteenth and fourteenth centuries, stands on the site of a Saxon church. In 1884 the parish magazine stated: 'The aisle and chancel of the church are full of bodies, and if, as is most probable, stones marked the places of interment, they ought certainly to have been raised on end outside the building (when the floor was laid with tiles), so that future generations might know something of the past.'

Town and Castle
Ludlow

The market town of Ludlow lies close to the Hereford and Worcester border, just east of the confluence of the rivers Teme and Corve. It grew up around the Norman castle and was designed on the grid-iron pattern of most medieval settlements. It was granted its first market charter in 1189 and prospered, primarily, on the wool trade. The church of St Laurence, with its massive 135-foot-high tower, dominates the town. The largest parish church in the county, it dates from the late twelfth century, was essentially rebuilt in the fifteenth century and later restored. In the town centre, at the top of Broad Street, is the Butter Cross, the upper floor of which was once used as the town hall and later as a charity school. It was built in 1743 by William Baker. The decorative, timber-framed Feathers Hotel, dating from 1603, is a fine example of a wealthy lawyer's private house. It was converted into an inn in 1670. The Old Bull Tavern on the opposite side of the street, although not so striking, is even older.

Ludlow Castle
Ludlow

Ludlow is not mentioned in the Domesday Book of 1086. But by the end of the century the Normans had built a castle of stone on the rocky cliff overlooking the Teme valley. Gilbert de Lacy altered and enlarged the structure during the latter half of the twelfth century. When Roger Mortimer, the powerful Marcher Lord, acquired the property in 1306, he began to transform the fortress into a palace. In 1472 it became the administrative centre of the Council for Wales and the Marches, set up by Edward IV to govern the whole of Wales and the border frontier. The king decided to send his young son, Edward, Prince of Wales, to Ludlow to act as a figurehead, along with his younger brother, Richard. After the princes had been murdered in the Tower of London on the orders of Richard of Gloucester, Henry VII resurrected the idea of the Council and sent his eldest son, Prince Arthur, to Ludlow. Although Arthur died in 1502, Ludlow continued as a centre for regional government until the end of the seventeenth century. The castle ruins are now in the care of the Earl of Powis.

Hereford and Herefordshire

Dinmore Manor
near Hereford

Midway between Hereford and Leominster, on a magnificent hilltop site set in over 1,000 acres of fields and woodland, stands Dinmore Manor and the Commandery of the Knights Hospitaller of St John of Jerusalem. The estate was purchased in 1927 by Richard Hollins Murray, inventor of the 'catseye' reflecting lenses, patented in 1923, which were subsequently developed by Percy Shaw into the self-wiping roadstud. In 1929–36 Murray added to the basically seventeenth-century manor house a Gothic-style Music Room (Great Hall), Cloisters and Grotto. The chapel and the Knights' Commandery were founded some time between 1163 and 1188 by Thomas de Dunemora. The grant was confirmed by Richard I in 1190 and again by King John 'in more ample terms' (Robinson). Thus enriched, it became the headquarters of the military and monastic Order of the Hospitallers in Herefordshire, with jurisdiction over dependent cells at Garway, Harewood, Rowlestone, Sutton St Michael, Upleadon and Wormbridge. By the Dissolution it had become one of the most important houses in England and Wales.

Like the Severn, the River Wye rises on the barren slopes of Plynlimon in the mountains of central Wales. Instead of flowing north-east into Shropshire, however, the Wye winds its way south-east, through Powys, Herefordshire, Gloucestershire and Gwent, to debouch into the tidal Severn at Beachley. Apart from the city of Hereford, the largest settlements it meets on its 154-mile-long journey are the small market towns of Builth Wells, Hay-on-Wye, Ross-on-Wye, Monmouth and Chepstow. After crossing the Welsh border at Hay-on-Wye, the river meanders in a series of long lazy loops, through the rich red soils of the Herefordshire plain (developed on Old Red Sandstone rocks) to the spectacular Carboniferous Limestone cliffs of Coldwell Rocks and Symonds Yat.

Ringed by hills – with the narrow spine of the Malverns forming a barrier in the east and the great escarpment of the Black Mountains of Wales in the west – and watered by the Wye, Lugg, Monnow, Frome, Arrow, Dore and Teme, Herefordshire is essentially an agricultural county. In 1804 Duncumb wrote that it 'exhibits altogether a scene of luxuriance and beauty, certainly not surpassed, perhaps not equalled, by any county of England.' Camden noted that it was renowned for its three Ws – wheat, wool and water. Many have praised its three Cs – corn, cattle and cider. While others, carried away by alphabetical contortions, claim that it is envied for its six Ws – wheat, wool, water, wood, women and wine (the latter being cider). Unquestionably, the rich red soil and lush pastureland of Herefordshire is ideally suited for the growing of crops and the breeding of animals.

In the 1720s Daniel Defoe remarked that the people of the county were 'diligent and laborious . . . chiefly addicted to husbandry, and they boast, perhaps, not without reason, that they have the finest wool, and the best hops, and the richest cider in all Britain.' Described as the 'orchard of England', Herefordshire (and indeed Worcestershire) produces dessert and cooking apples, plums, damsons, pears and cherries for the markets of the region. But the county is particularly renowned for its cider, as Edward Davies acknowledged in 1786:

> No better cider does the world supply,
> Than grows along thy borders, gentle Wye.
> Deliciously strong and exquisitely fine,
> With all the friendly properties of wine.

Made from the juices, usually blended, of small, hard and bitter apples like Redstreak, Bitter-Sweet, Brown Snout, Kingston Black and Foxwhelp, most of the county's cider is now produced in large factories at Hereford, Stoke Lacy and Much Marcle. However, smaller, traditional cider-makers do still exist.

Perry, a less-lauded drink, is produced from the juice of crushed perry pears. Pre-dating cider, which was essentially a medieval drink, perry is known to have been drunk, at least as far back as Roman times. Although it has a reputation for its potency, John Beale in the seventeenth century considered that it was fit only for women: 'Pears make a weak drink fit for our hinds, and is generally refused by our gentry as breeding wind in the stomach.' Another drink-making crop, grown along the Teme valley and south of Ledbury, is hops, used as a bitter-flavouring ingredient in the brewing of beer.

'The cattle of Herefordshire have long been esteemed superior to most, if not all, the breeds in the island,' observed Duncumb. 'Those of Devonshire and Sussex approach nearest to them in general appearance. Large size, an athletic form, and unusual neatness, characterize the true sort: the prevailing colour is a reddish brown, with white faces.' Today Hereford cattle, famed not only for their beef but also for their hardiness, can be found in most countries throughout the world.

During the nineteenth century the predominant breed of sheep in the county was Ryeland, bred from the original Hereford, which was renowned for its soft, dense wool. 'They are small, white faced, and hornless,' noted Duncumb. 'In symmetry of shape, and in the flavour of their meat, they are superior to most flocks in England; in the quality of their wool, they are wholly unrivalled.' Around Leominster the wool was so highly valued that it came to be known as 'Lempster ore'.

Before the arrival of the railways in the 1850s, most of the produce of the Herefordshire countryside was shipped down the Wye to the 'Severn-Sea' – from where it made its way to ports like Bristol and London – or sold in the markets of Bromyard, Leominster, Kington, Ross-on-Wye, Ledbury and Hereford. From little more than a satellite settlement on the Roman city of Magnis (Kenchester), a few miles to the north-west, Hereford became a bishopric, a Saxon shire town, a fortified city, a river port and an administrative capital. Today, although it has some industries, it remains essentially an agricultural centre, serving the needs of the surrounding rural farming communities.

Green Man Inn
Fownhope

Fownhope lies on rising ground above the River Wye, 6 miles south-east of Hereford. During the seventeenth and eighteenth centuries the village depended for much of its trade on river-barge traffic. The Heart of Oak Friendly Society still celebrates the 'Club Walk' on or around Oak Apple Day (29 May), in which members carry club-sticks decorated with flowers to the church. The event always finishes at the fifteenth-century Green Man Inn. Originally called the 'Naked Boy', the timber-framed inn was once used as a court-house. Thomas Winter, boxing champion of England 1823–4 and professionally known as Tom Spring, was born at Ridge End Farm. The parish church of St Mary, one of the largest in the county, has a square Norman tower and shingled oak spire. Inside, set in the west wall, is the tympanum of a twelfth-century doorway depicting the Virgin and Child with a lion and eagle. Outside the churchyard wall are the remains of a whipping post and the old village stocks. Nearby is a surprisingly accurate milestone, erected in 1907. On the wooded hills to the north and south of the village are the earthwork remains of two pre-Roman camps.

Croft Castle
near Leominster

The Domesday Book of 1086 records that the manor of 'Crofta', was held by Bernard de Croft under William de Scohies (or Schoies). The Croft family have held the estate ever since, except for an intermission of 177 years (between 1746 and 1923). The destiny of the family was long tied up with the fortunes of their powerful neighbours the Mortimers of Wigmore, Earls of March. Sir Richard Croft, whose wife was widow of a Mortimer, fought at the Battle of Mortimer's Cross in February 1461, in which the Lancastrians were defeated by the Yorkist army of Edward Mortimer, Earl of March (shortly to become Edward IV). The battle was incidentally waged on Croft land. Originally a Marcher castle, built to defend the family's rights and property in a region torn by border warfare, Croft Castle was gradually transformed from a fortress to a country house. Roughly square in plan with a tower in each corner, it is thought to date from the fourteenth century. Modifications continued over succeeding centuries, with the addition of a battlemented porch in 1913. Just east of the castle is the Church of St Michael, dating from the fourteenth century.

Berrington Hall
near Leominster

Three miles north of Leominster, just east of Eye Manor, Berrington Hall is set in extensive parkland with an uninterrupted view across the Herefordshire countryside to the Black Mountains of Wales. The house, essentially rectangular in design, with a high portico on the West Front supported by four unfluted Ionic columns, was built by Henry Holland for the Rt Hon. Thomas Harley in 1778–81. Its brick core was faced with a reddish sandstone, quarried from Shuttocks Hill, about a mile distant. In order to transport the stone from the quarry, a horse tramway was specially constructed. It is thought that the site for the house was chosen with the advice of Lancelot 'Capability' Brown, the architect's father-in-law. Harley commissioned Brown to landscape the grounds, and his designs included a 14-acre lake, or 'pool', with a 4-acre island. The interior of the house, in contrast to the relatively simple exterior, is strikingly lavish, with a magnificent staircase hall and finely decorated ceilings. Berrington Hall was purchased by the Cawley family in 1900 and came into the care of the National Trust in 1957.

Bunns Croft Cottage
Moreton

On the road between Ashton and
Luston, north-west of Berrington
Hall, are two small farming
hamlets, known as Moreton and
Eye. Moreton lies on the edge of
Berrington Park and contains a
number of attractive timber-framed
cottages. It has no shops or public
house. The derelict canal nearby
was part of a waterway, projected
in 1790, linking Stourport with
Leominster and Kington. The
manor of Eye was held by the de
Eye family, under the Abbot of
Reading, from the reign of Henry
III to that of Henry VI. It was
purchased in 1673 by Ferdinando
Gorges, a Barbados sugar and slave
trader, who died in 1701. The
present red-brick Eye Manor,
which is noted for its decorated
plaster ceilings, is dated 1680.
From 1817 until 1912 it was the
vicarage. The reddish-grey
sandstone church of St Peter and St
Paul, serving both hamlets, dates
from around 1190. The west tower,
with its stair turret, was mostly
rebuilt in 1874 by W. Chick. The
church contains a pulpit, dated
1681, with carved figures and
several monuments to the
Cornewall family, who owned the
Berrington estate in medieval times.
Traces of the family's fortified
manor can be found one mile east of
Moreton, near Ashton.

River Arrow
Eardisland

The River Arrow flows through the
village of Eardisland before
winding its way east to join the
Lugg, a short distance south-east of
Leominster. Many of its houses and
cottages are pleasantly situated on
either bank of the river. The timber-
framed, old schoolhouse, built in
1652, stands on the south side of
the bridge. It ceased to be a school
in 1825 and has now been
converted into two private
dwellings: Millstream and Bridge
Cottages. Attached to the exterior
of the latter is a whipping post. In
the grounds of the manor house,
dating from the seventeenth
century, is a tall, four-gabled brick
dovecote. All that is left of the
moated castle is a tree-clad mound,
near the church. On the north bank
of the river is Staick House, an
impressive timber-framed mansion,
dating from about 1300. A lane
running south from the village leads
to Burton Court, a large country
house, rebuilt in Regency times
around an early fourteenth-century
great hall. The neo-Tudor front,
designed by Sir Clough Williams-
Ellis, dates from 1912. It is open
to visitors.

Grange Court
Leominster

Merewald, King of Mercia, founded a monastery at Leominster in about AD 660. It was destroyed by Danes in the ninth century, replaced by a collegiate church, later re-founded as a nunnery and suppressed in 1046. The present parish church, remarkable for its three naves, was the former Benedictine priory church, founded in c. 1125 by Henry I. Inside is a medieval ducking stool, last used in 1809. From medieval times until the eighteenth century, Leominster, on the west bank of the River Lugg, was a noted centre for the wool trade. Today it remains a busy market town, selling livestock and agricultural produce from the surrounding countryside. Grange Court, built in 1633 by John Abel, the 'King's Carpenter', was formerly the town hall. Originally sited at the junction of Burgess Street and Broad Street, it was deemed a traffic hazard and sold by auction in 1853. Resold the same day, it was dismantled and re-erected on the green near the church as a private residence. In 1938–9, to prevent its export to the USA, it was purchased by the then Borough Council and has been used as offices ever since.

West Street
Pembridge

Pembridge, on the south bank of the River Arrow, was granted a market charter in 1240 by Henry III. It prospered as a major trading centre for the surrounding area until the nineteenth century. The Market Hall, supported by eight oak pillars, dates from the early sixteenth century and originally had an upper storey. The village has many examples of black-and-white timber-framed buildings, the earliest dating from the fourteenth century. These include the Court House Farm (which occupies the site of a moated castle or manor house), the New Inn (dating from 1311), Ye Olde Steppes (formerly the Rectory), the early sixteenth-century Pembridge Inn, the Duppa's Almshouses (founded in 1661) and the Trafford Almshouses (founded in 1686). Although the church of St Mary the Virgin has Norman fragments, it was mainly built between 1320 and 1360. Work was delayed because of the shortage of labour caused by the 1349 plague. Dating from the same century is the detached, pagoda-like Bell Tower, said to be structurally related to a Scandinavian style adopted in Essex, rather than in the Marches!

Market Pitch
Weobley

At Weobley – between the parish
church of St Peter and St Paul and
the earthwork remains of the
Norman castle – is a wealth of
timber-framed buildings, many
between 400 and 600 years old.
Situated some 10 miles north-west
of Hereford, the village is
mentioned in the Domesday Book.
It became a market town and an
important borough, returning two
Members of Parliament before the
1832 Reform Bill (Weobley was
one of fifty-six 'rotten' English
boroughs which were
disenfranchized by the Bill). Its
early prosperity was based on ale-
making and glove-manufacture.
During the eighteenth century it
gained notoriety as a centre for
witchcraft. Inside the church is a
life-size white marble statue of
Colonel John Birch (1615–91). A
staunch Parliamentarian, soldier
and MP, he was one of the
signatories on Charles I's death
warrant. In the mid-nineteenth
century around forty houses were
demolished in the main street,
including the market hall. The few
that were left were destroyed by fire
in 1943. The facia boards on Ye
Olde Salutation Inn, in Market
Pitch, came from the fire-gutted
buildings.

Lower Brockhampton
near Bromyard

Dating from the end of the
fourteenth century, the moated
timber-framed manor house at
Lower Brockhampton is buried in
remote wooded countryside, some
2 miles east of Bromyard. It was
built by John Domulton, a
descendant of the Brockhampton
family who lived here from at least
the twelfth century. The moat
which originally surrounded the
property now only survives on
three sides. Bridging the moat is an
attractive detached timber-framed
gatehouse, erected in the late
fifteenth century; its projecting
upper storey seems to balance
precariously on the lower, through
which access is gained to the grassy
court. Although the manor house
may have been reduced in size
(some believe that it had a west
wing, similar to the east) the Great
Hall with its fine timber roof
survives. Part of the property was
carefully rebuilt in the 1870s by
J. C. Buckler. The roofless ruins of
a Norman chapel, built of soft
porous tufa probably by the
Brockhamptons in about 1180, can
be found in the farmyard to the
west of the house. The 2,000-acre
Brockhampton Park estate was
bequeathed to the National Trust
in 1946.

Church Lane
Ledbury

The narrow, cobbled Church Lane – connecting the churchyard of St Michael and All Saints with the seventeenth-century Market House – contains a number of black-and-white timber-framed houses, some with overhangs. The Old Grammar School, dating from 1480–1520, and the sixteenth-century Butcher Row House (re-erected here in 1979) are now both museums. The Prince of Wales inn, with another entrance in Church Street, dates from the fifteenth and sixteenth centuries. Many of the houses in the centre of Ledbury date from the sixteenth and seventeenth centuries, when the cloth and leather industries brought prosperity to the market town. Some of the houses were re-fronted during the eighteenth century, when brick became the fashion. Near the 'really terrible' (Pevsner) Barrett Browning Institute, opened in 1896, are the almshouses of St Katherine's Hospital, first founded in 1232. Despite being rebuilt in 1822 and 1866, the fourteenth-century chapel survives. Ledbury Park, built by the Biddulph family in about 1590, is 'the grandest black and white house in the county' (Pevsner).

The Old House
Hereford

Built in 1621, the Old House at the east end of High Town was originally part of a continuous street frontage, known as Butchers' Row. This timber-framed row of buildings, where animals were slaughtered and meat sold, replaced the earlier less-permanent stalls of market traders. Adjacent to the three-gabled Old House was the George Inn. By 1837 the entire row, except for the Old House, had been demolished; the last to survive being Caswall's cutlery shop. During much of the nineteenth century the Old House was a saddlery and tackle shop. By 1879, however, the main part of the building was in use as a hardware shop, with a fishmongers adjoining. The shop-keeper and his family lived on the upper floors. In about 1882 the three-storeyed house became a branch of the Worcester City and County Bank, who restored the building and inserted windows in the east and west sides. Lloyd's Bank, who eventually acquired the property, presented it to the City in 1928. Now one of Hereford's museums, the house contains a fascinating collection of seventeenth-century furniture.

Hereford Cathedral
Hereford

The see of Hereford, one of the oldest in England, was founded in 676, when Putta of Rochester became its first bishop. In 794 Ethelbert, King of East Anglia, journeyed to Offa's palace at Sutton Walls, 4 miles north of the city, intending to marry the Mercian king's daughter, Alfrida. Ethelbert, however, was beheaded by Offa and his body taken to Hereford for burial. After a spate of miracles had occurred at his tomb, Ethelbert was canonized. The city and church subsequently prospered, partly from the benefactions of the Mercian kings and partly from the multitudes drawn to the martyred king's shrine. In 1012 Bishop Athelstan commenced the building of a grander church, but this was destroyed by the Welsh in 1055. Although often credited to Bishop Reinhelm (1107–15), the present cathedral was begun by the Norman Bishop Robert de Losinga in 1079. Alterations and additions have continued over the centuries, with major rebuilding after the collapse of the west tower in 1786. Dedicated to St Mary and St Ethelbert, the cathedral is noted for its medieval library, with about 1,500 chained books and the famous Mappa Mundi map.

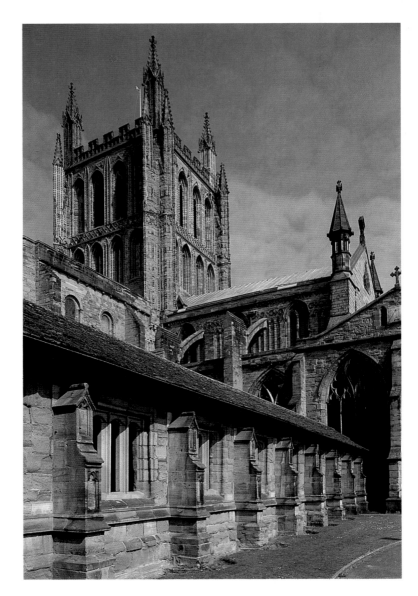

St Cuthbert's Church
Holme Lacy

Standing on low-lying ground, above the green water-meadows of the River Wye, the church of St Cuthbert is sited about a mile away from the present village centre. It was originally built in about 1280, although most of the present structure is fourteenth century. Holme Lacy (formerly Hamme) takes the latter part of its name from Walter de Lacy, who received the manor from the Bishop of Hereford during the reign of William I. It belonged to the de Lacy family until the fourteenth century, when it passed to the Scudamores. Holme Lacy House, set in extensive grounds, was built for the 2nd Viscount Scudamore during the 1670s. For centuries the landowners or 'brinkers', whose property adjoined the river, claimed the right to fish in the 'free waters' between Holme Lacy and Strangford. This right was challenged in the early twentieth century by the Earl of Chesterfield (the then owner of Holme Lacy House). After a bitter legal battle, the case was settled by the House of Lords in 1911, in favour of the earl. Just north-east of the village, the Wye is joined by the waters of the Lugg and Frome.

St Mary's Church
Abbey Dore

Founded in 1147 for Cistercian
monks from Morimond by Robert
FitzHarold, Earl of Ferrers and
Lord of Ewyas, Abbey Dore was
dedicated to the Blessed Virgin
Mary. Rebuilding began in about
1180 and continued until about
1260. Lying to the west of the
county, at the southern end of
Golden Valley, the abbey was often
troubled by raiders from across the
Welsh border and was attacked and
damaged in 1371. In 1540, after the
Dissolution, the abbey estate was
granted to John Scudamore of
Holme Lacy, who acquired the
rectory and tithes at a later date.
Services, however, continued to be
held in the church and transepts,
despite the poor state of the
wooden roof. The former monastic
building was restored in 1633 by
John Viscount Scudamore for use
as a parish church. This included
the addition of the tower. Further
restoration was carried out
between 1895 and 1904. During
the summer the church is the roost
for one of the largest Natterer's bat
colonies in England. On the
opposite bank of the River Dore to
the church is Abbey Dore Court
gardens, open throughout the
summer.

Goodrich Castle
Goodrich

Commanding an ancient crossing
of the Wye, over 100 feet above the
river, Goodrich Castle was first
recorded in a document of about
1101, under the name 'Godric's
Castle'. Godric was almost
certainly Godric of Mappestone,
mentioned in the Domesday Book
of 1086. Originally built of earth
and timber on the summit of a spur
of red sandstone, the fortress was
rebuilt in stone in the mid-twelfth
century with a strong three-
storeyed keep. Although it was
largely rebuilt again in the late
thirteenth century by the Earls of
Pembroke, the keep was retained.
The entrance was doubly guarded
by a barbican and gatehouse. For
several centuries it was the
principal home of the Talbots, who
were created Earls of Shrewsbury in
the fifteenth century. It was
besieged by the Parliamentarians
during the Civil War and, after the
Royalists under Sir Henry Lingen
had been forced to surrender
through lack of water, it was
partially demolished. The castle
was sold in 1740 by the Earl of
Kent, whose family came into the
property after the Talbots had left.
It subsequently passed through
various ownerships and is now in
the care of English Heritage.

Gloucester and North-Western Gloucestershire

Mill Avon Waterfront
Tewkesbury

According to Rudder, Tewkesbury is situated 'in a rich vale . . . watered by four rivers, like the garden of Eden.' The rivers are the Severn, its tributary the Avon and the two small streams, the Swilgate and the Carrant Brook, which flow into the Avon, one at either end of the town. 'The water is out at Tewkesbury' is a local saying which refers to the fact that after heavy and continuous rain the rivers are liable to flood the surrounding meadows. Particularly vulnerable is The Ham, the wide expanse of common land lying between the Severn and Avon. The Avon divides near King John's Bridge: the Old Avon takes the short route west to the Severn, while the Mill Avon, probably cut by the monks in the twelfth century to power Abbey Mill, continues south to enter the Severn near Bloody Meadow, the site of the 1471 battle. Healing's Mill, built in 1865 by Samuel Healing, was rebuilt in 1976 and is one of the largest inland flour mills in England, still receiving some of its grain by barge from Gloucester Docks. Abbey Mill was rebuilt in 1793 and did not finally cease working until after the First World War.

'Gloucester,' wrote Randall in 1862, 'with its cathedral, its railways, its warehouses, its docks, and its fleet of vessels, is now before us. The latter, no longer confined to the tight-rigged craft of the Severn, include vessels that brave the deep, and that bring the flags of nations within its walls; whilst custom-houses, sea stores, and merchandise are met with, that give it the aspect of a sea-port rather than of an inland town.' As a thriving commercial port, the city owed its prosperity to the construction of the 16-mile-long Gloucester and Sharpness Canal, completed in 1827 and designed to bypass the river hazards of the lower Severn. As Britain's export trade expanded, however, so the ships grew in size and by the 1860s the ocean-going vessels were too large to navigate the canal. Although new docks were built at Sharpness, it was Bristol, having also expanded its dock-system, that attracted the seaborne trade, and Gloucester rapidly declined. In recent years, however, the Victorian dockland area of Gloucester has undergone considerable redevelopment as a centre for tourists and boating enthusiasts, with restaurants, public houses, workshops, warehouses and museums.

Gloucester's development from the Roman fortified city of Glevum to the capital of the Anglo-Saxon kingdom of Mercia and then to county capital owes much to its position on the River Severn. Situated in the broad vale between the Cotswold escarpment and the Forest of Dean at the lowest crossing-point of the river, the city depended for much of its trade on the waterway network of which the Severn was the main artery. During the nineteenth century barges from Gloucester and Bristol could reach as far upstream as Shrewsbury, even Welshpool. Today, however, the recommended upper limit for navigation is Stourport-on-Severn.

The Severn, 220 miles in length, is the longest river in Britain. It rises on Plynlimon in the mountains of central Wales and flows in a huge semi-circular curve through Shropshire, Worcestershire, Gloucestershire and Avon to the sea. Counted among its seventeen tributaries are the Vyrnwy, Perry, Tern, Stour, Salwarpe, Teme, Avon, Frome and Wye. These, and the bulk of the region's rivers, flow south to debouch into the Atlantic Ocean, via the Severn and the Bristol Channel. The Trent, however, with its tributaries the Derwent, Dove, Tame and Soar, flows north to enter the North Sea via the Humber. The Heart of England is essentially a vast and fertile plain, watered by numerous rivers and streams, most of whose origins — unlike the Severn — lie amidst smooth sloping hills. Because so much of the landscape is broad and flat, extensive tracts of it are susceptible to severe flooding. Settlements, therefore, tend to be sited on higher less vulnerable ground, with fields, orchards and market-gardens occupying the gently falling valley floors.

When the land was undeveloped, covered by dense forests and undrained marshland, the rivers were seen not as barriers but as highways and in many cases the sole means by which any communication and trade could be carried out. Since ancient times England's heartland has been crisscrossed by a network of roads, including those constructed by the Romans – Watling Street, Ryknild Street, Buckle Street and the Fosse Way. Nevertheless, the slow sluggish rivers, characteristic of the region, were found to be ideally suited for the transportation of heavy and bulky goods. Throughout the seventeenth century many rivers were canalized or made navigable: the Avon from Stratford to Tewkesbury, for instance, was opened to river-traffic in 1636–9. In the 1660s work began on making the Stour navigable from Stourport-on-Severn to Stourbridge, from where a 46-mile-long canal was later constructed to join the Trent. The insatiable demand for coal to fuel what was to become the Industrial Revolution led to a rapid expansion of the canal network: the first part of the Shropshire Union Canal was opened in 1774, the Trent and Mersey Canal was completed in 1777, the Coventry Canal was finished in 1790, the Stratford-upon-Avon Canal was opened in its entirety in 1814, while the Worcester and Birmingham Canal was opened in 1815.

The arrival of the railways in the mid-nineteenth century, sadly, heralded the decline of the commercial waterways. Complex navigation systems, which had been effectively maintained since the early seventeenth century, deteriorated rapidly, and consequently the rivers and canals became impassable. During the 1950s, however, to cite one example, work began on the colossal task of restoring the River Avon to its former navigable condition. On 1 June 1974 the final stage was accomplished with the opening of a new river-lock at Stratford-upon-Avon by Queen Elizabeth, the Queen Mother. During the ceremony Sir John Betjeman, the Poet Laureate, addressed Her Majesty, concluding with the triumphant confirmation that with the re-opening of the lock, she had 'set free' / The heart of England to the open sea.'

Gloucester Cathedral
Gloucester

The abbey of St Peter at Gloucester was founded as a double house for monks and nuns in about 681 by Osric, one of King Ethelred of Mercia's ministers or viceroys. Encouraged by Wolstan, Bishop of Worcester, King Canute made it a Benedictine abbey for monks in 1022. Destroyed by fire, it was rebuilt in 1058 by Aldred, Bishop of Worcester. After the Norman Conquest, Abbot Serlo commenced another rebuilding programme, but on a much grander scale, with the main body of construction taking place between 1089 and 1260. During this time the abbey suffered from further fires but was never totally destroyed. Restorations, alterations and additions continued through to the fifteenth century, when the South Porch (pictured here) and massive 225-foot-high Perpendicular tower were erected. After the dissolution of the abbey, it was refounded in 1541 by Henry VIII as a cathedral, dedicated to the Holy Trinity. Rudder noted in 1779: 'At the dissolution of the abbey . . . it had the good fortune to be so entirely preserved, that no conventual church in the kingdom, except that of Westminster, escaped so well.' Edward II and Robert, Duke of Normandy, are among those buried in the church.

Westbury Court Garden
Westbury-on-Severn

Before it was given to the National Trust in 1967 the garden at Westbury Court was an overgrown wilderness, smothered with a dense jungle of nettles and brambles. A programme of restoration, based on the original account books and an engraving by Kip of about 1707, has transformed the 5-acre site into one of the rarest surviving water gardens of its type in England. Originally laid out between 1696 and 1705 by Colonel Maynard Colchester in the fashionable formal Dutch style of the period, the garden contained a narrow Long Canal, 450 feet long and 22 feet wide. The T-Canal is thought to have been added by Colchester's nephew, Maynard Colchester II. In the centre of its junction is a stone statue of Neptune astride a dolphin. It probably dates from the mid-seventeenth century and, traditionally, was rescued from the Severn after being found embedded in mud at low tide. Westbury Court Garden is located in water meadows on the north bank of the river, 8 miles south-west of Gloucester. A similar water garden at Charlecote, Warwickshire, was destroyed by Capability Brown in the eighteenth century.

Coppet Hill and River Wye
Symonds Yat

Thirteen miles downstream of Ross-on-Wye (less than half that distance as the crow flies), the River Wye makes a great loop around Huntsham Hill, before winding south to Monmouth, Chepstow and the Severn. Some 500 feet above the loop, on the western fringes of the Forest of Dean, is Symonds Yat Rock, with spectacular views in all directions. Situated on the Hereford/Gloucester border, just inside Gloucestershire, the rock is thought to take its name from Robert Symonds, High Sheriff of Herefordshire in the seventeenth century. Yat is derived from the Old English *geat*, meaning gap or gate (which refers to the pass through the hills along the Wye valley). The place is extremely popular, especially with bird-watchers, as it is the haunt and nesting site of peregrine falcons. The river can be crossed by ferry at the Saracen's Head Hotel and Ye Olde Ferrie Inne. On Little Doward hill, to the west, are the earthwork remains of an Iron Age hill-fort. In nearby King Arthur's Cave, 200 feet above the river, the bones of prehistoric animals like the mammoth, hyena, bear and rhinoceros have been discovered. Offa's Dyke runs along the steep edge of the wooded plateau.

Tithe Barn
Ashleworth

Standing on the west bank of the
Severn, 6 miles north of Gloucester,
is an attractive group of medieval
stone buildings – church, house and
tithe barn – which once belonged to
St Augustine's Abbey, Bristol. The
church is mainly fifteenth century
but contains herringbone masonry
dating from as early as about 1100.
The Court House was built in about
1460. The tithe barn, 125 feet long
and 25 feet wide with two
projecting porches, dates from
about 1500. It is one of a number of
tithe barns in the region owned by
the National Trust. Bredon Barn, 3
miles north-east of Tewkesbury,
was built for the Bishops of
Worcester in the mid-fourteenth
century. Measuring 132 feet by 44
feet, it has been extensively restored
after a fire in 1980. Although it has
been traditionally known as a tithe
barn, recent research has
established that it was almost
certainly a manorial barn,
belonging to the manor of Bredon.
Tithe barns were attached to
churches and were used to store
tithes (one tenth of the produce of
the land) paid to parish priests as
part of their income. The 140-foot-
long Middle Littleton tithe barn, 3
miles north-east of Evesham, may
date from about 1260.

The Docks
Gloucester

During medieval times Gloucester
was a thriving inland port with a
seaborne trade in wool, leather and
grain. The availability of iron ore,
coal and timber from the nearby
Forest of Dean encouraged
blacksmiths and iron-workers to
settle in the city, and by the
fourteenth century there was a bell-
founding industry. In 1827
Gloucester was linked by a 16-mile-
long ship canal to Sharpness docks
and the Bristol Channel. Although
seaborne trade has markedly
declined, the canal is still used by
coasters, pleasure craft and ships
not larger than 190 feet by 29 feet,
with a maximum draught of 10
feet. Headroom is unlimited as all
the bridges were made to open,
either manually or by power-
assisted means. The redevelopment
of the Victorian dockland at
Gloucester in recent years has
included the restoration of the
surrounding brick warehouses, one
of which now houses the National
Waterways Museum. Exhibits
inside the seven-storey Llanthony
Warehouse, with its cast-iron
columns and timber floors,
illustrate the story of Britain's
canals. Among the museum's
growing collection of floating
exhibits is the S.N.D. No. 4
steam dredger.

St Mary's Church
Deerhurst

Three miles south-west of Tewkesbury, on the east bank of the Severn, Deerhurst was described by Leland in about 1540: 'The site of the town, as it is now, is in a manner of a meadow. So that when Severn much riseth the water cometh almost about the town. It is supposed that it was of old time less subject to waters, and that the bottom of Severn, then deeper without choking of sands, did at floods less hurt.' Even today, the floodwaters of the river come right up to the churchyard walls. During Saxon times Deerhurst was an important monastic centre, with a priory said to have been founded in about 715. Destroyed by the Danes in about 975, it was rebuilt and refounded by Edward the Confessor sometime before 1059. He gave it to the Abbey of St Denis in France, and after various ownerships it became a cell of Tewkesbury Abbey in 1467, remaining so until the Dissolution. One of the largest Saxon buildings in England, with later additions, St Mary's is now the parish church of the village. The east claustral range, adjoining, is now a private house. Odda's Chapel, close by, was built by Earl Odda in 1056. It is now in the care of English Heritage.

Imperial Square
Cheltenham

In 1779, according to Rudder, the ancient market town of Cheltenham consisted 'of one handsome street, near a mile long. The buildings are chiefly of brick. It is situated on the border of a fine fertile vale, about two miles from Cleeve, Prestbury, and Leckhampton hills, which join the Cotswolds, and forming a kind of semi-circle, defend the town from those cold blasts which proceed from the eastern quarter.' Although the properties of its spa waters had been discovered and exploited earlier that century, the town was not to become fashionable until George III's five-week visit in 1788. Over the next three decades the population of the town multiplied sevenfold, culminating in the large-scale development of a brand new town, planned on classical lines, with broad tree-lined streets and open spaces – the first 'Garden City' in England. The neo-Greek style of architecture, with its attractive use of decorative ironwork, continued well into the 1840s. The balconies of the elegant terraced houses in Imperial Square, for example, are decorated with 'double heart' patterned ironwork, common throughout the town.

The Pittville Pump Room
Cheltenham

The Pittville Estate, on the north side of Cheltenham, was created by Joseph Pitt, lawyer, banker and MP. Working with the local architect John Forbes, he published the plans for his new development in 1826. It was never fully realized. The Pittville Pump Room, partly modelled on the Temple of Ilissus in Athens, was completed in 1830 and is considered by some to be the 'finest gem' of Cheltenham's Regency architecture. Sir Hugh Casson, however, called it 'stilted, high shouldered and rather graceless.' Set in an attractive park, above the ornamental lake, it consists of a great central hall, surmounted by a gallery and dome, with an impressive colonnade of Ionic columns. Waters can still be sampled from the original spa fountain. The upper floors are now a museum, featuring the Gallery of Fashion, while concerts are held in the hall. Today, the spa town is famous for its international festivals of music and literature and for sporting events like the Cheltenham Gold Cup steeplechase and the Gloucestershire Cricket Festival, first held in 1872. It is also the birthplace of Gustav Holst (1874–1934).

Tewkesbury Abbey
Tewkesbury

Tewkesbury takes its name from Theoc, a seventh-century hermit, who lived in a hut near the confluence of the rivers Avon and Severn. In 715 the Mercian dukes, Odda and Dodda, founded a small monastery on the site. Little more is known about the monastery until the ninth century, when it was ravaged by Danish invaders and twice destroyed by fire. It declined so much in importance that in 980 it became a cell of the newly founded Benedictine monastery at Cranborne in Dorset. Tewkesbury Abbey was founded in 1092 by Robert FitzHamon and Giraldus, Abbot of Cranborne, occupied in 1102 and consecrated in 1121. In 1540, at the Dissolution, it had become one of the wealthiest religious houses in England. The church was condemned as superfluous and ordered to be demolished, but the townsfolk persuaded Henry VIII to sell them the abbey church and churchyard for £453, the estimated value of the lead on the roof and the metal from the bells. The 148-foot-high tower originally supported a lead-covered wooden spire, some 100 feet high. It collapsed in 1559 during a gale and was never replaced. The pinnacles were added in 1660.

Worcester and Worcestershire

Main Street
Elmley Castle

Nestling on the northern wooded slopes of Bredon Hill, Elmley Castle has been labelled 'one of the ten prettiest villages in England'. It contains a number of attractive black-and-white timbered cottages, three public houses, a cider mill and a pottery. Elmley is derived from the elm tree and the Anglo-Saxon word *leah*, and means 'the elm by the rough pasture land'. The great elms were killed by Dutch elm disease in the 1970s. The church of St Mary dates from the eleventh and twelfth centuries and contains various memorials to the Savage family, who purchased the manor in 1544. They lived in the mansion by the church until the early nineteenth century. During the reign of Henry III (1216–72) the inhabitants of the village were granted the right to hold a market and fair. Evidence of this can be seen in the wide main street, leading to the church, and the stone cross at the entrance to the village. The castle, standing high on the slopes of the hill above the village, was built shortly after the Norman Conquest, but by the early fourteenth century it was in ruins.

In her Journal of 1698 Celia Fiennes wrote:

Worcester town is washed by the River Severn. It's a large city, 12 churches, the streets most of them broad, the buildings some of them are very good and lofty. It's encompassed with a wall which has 4 gates that are very strong. The Market Place is large. There is a Guildhall besides the Market House which stands on pillars of stone. The Cathedral stands in a large yard pitched, it's a lofty magnificent building.

At the time of Fiennes' visit the construction material of all the substantial buildings in Worcester was stone, timber or brick. The Cathedral, although roofed with slate, lead and timber, made use of several varieties of stone, including pale oolitic limestone from the Cotswolds, soft red sandstone from Alveley and Highley in Shropshire, and hard, glossy dark-grey marble from Purbeck in Dorset.

Throughout the Heart of England, however, most of the buildings were built, not of imported materials, but of those that were local and readily accessible. Within the region there was (and still is) an abundant supply of stone, including several varieties of sandstone and a number of different types of limestone. These occur in specific locations, and inevitably the smaller buildings in the vicinity of each quarry tended to reflect the type of stone available. (The owners and builders of larger houses and churches usually felt that it was worthwhile to transport stone from more distant sites.)

In most of Worcestershire, the low-lying plain of Shropshire north and east of the Severn, southern Staffordshire and large areas of Warwickshire the underlying rock is essentially New Red Sandstone, a soft reddish-brown stone that weathers comparatively badly. Among the larger structures built of this distinctive stone are Worcester and Lichfield Cathedrals and Kenilworth Castle; while towns like Warwick and Bridgnorth stand on outcrops of the rock. Wroxeter Roman City was built of sandstone from Grinshill in Shropshire, which had two pits, one producing red stone and the other greyish-white. Attingham Hall, and many buildings in Shrewsbury, also make use of this stone. Additionally, some varieties of sandstone, particularly in Herefordshire and Shropshire, can be easily split to produce slates for roofs. The pinkish, harder-to-cut Old Red Sandstone can be seen in the walls of houses and churches in western Worcestershire, throughout Herefordshire and in parts of south-western Shropshire. While carboniferous sandstone, quarried from Coal Measures, makes its appearance in buildings in and around the industrial West Midlands.

Although a grey type of sandstone occurs in the Forest of Dean, the most important building stone in Gloucestershire is oolitic limestone. Depending on its place of origin, the stone varies in colour from creamy white to dark brown. Gloucester Cathedral, for example, is built of a silver-grey limestone quarried at Painswick. While in the south-eastern corner of Worcestershire, around Broadway, the stone is a deep golden colour. Another type of limestone, pale and yellowy-grey, can be found around Wenlock Edge in Shropshire. This stone was used to build Wenlock Priory and many of the older houses in Much Wenlock.

Timber, however, was far more plentiful than stone, with broadleaved woodlands carpeting vast tracts of the midland plain. A significant number of today's villages and towns originated as clearings in forests like Feckenham, Wyre, Brewood, Clee, Clun and Arden. Much of this woodland has disappeared – felled for timber or fuel – and lives on only in the names of places.

The simplest types of timber building were constructed on a 'cruck' frame, made from a single curved trunk, split through the centre to produce two equal halves, or 'blades'. These were pegged together to form an arched support for the basic structure. In a small cottage two pairs of 'crucks' would be used, one at each end of the building, with a 'bay' between, usually about 16 feet in length, sometimes as little as 9. At first, each 'blade' reached down to the ground, but later they were supported on stone foundations. As builders became more confident, the timber frame became more complicated and the structures larger, more decorative and ambitious. For a rough guide to their age, the closer and thicker the timbers, the older the building.

The commonest roof-covering was thatch, but it proved to be a major fire hazard, especially in towns, and was invariably replaced by slates or tiles. The spaces between the wall timbers were filled with a variety of materials, including wattle-and-daub, woven slats of wood, and brick (clay for the latter being available in the broad river valleys). During the last few hundred years improvements in Britain's transportation network significantly diluted regional differences in building styles and materials, making houses much the same all over the country. Yet, for its rich diversity of local and traditional architecture, few regions can rival the Heart of England.

Pershore Abbey
Pershore

First founded for secular canons in about 689 by Oswald, nephew of Ethelred, King of Mercia, Pershore Abbey was refounded in 972 for Benedictine monks by King Edgar and Egelward, Duke of Dorset. The monks were ejected from the abbey shortly after Edgar's death in 975, probably by Alderman Aelfhere of Mercia. The monks were reinstated in 983, however, when Aelfhere suffered a horrible death, being eaten alive by worms or lice. Aelfhere's grandson was Earl Odda, who founded the Saxon chapel at Deerhurst in the memory of his brother, Aelfric. He was a benefactor of Pershore Abbey and is reputed to have purchased some of the bones of St Eadburga for the monastery. Dedicated to St Mary and St Eadburga, the abbey lost much of its lands when Edward the Confessor gave them to Westminster Abbey. The monks retaliated by closing the abbey church to Westminster's tenants in the town. To avoid further aggravation, the monks of Westminster built St Andrew's church, close by. The abbey was dissolved in 1540, and all that now survives is the choir, tower and south transept of the church and the almonry.

Bridge Cottage
Childswickham

On the northern fringes of the Cotswolds, just 2 miles north-west of Broadway, is Childswickham, nestling in the Vale of Evesham, surrounded by market gardens and fertile farmland. This ancient village, dating back to pre-Saxon times, contains a variety of houses and cottages, ranging from weathered red-brick to honey-coloured limestone to black-and-white half-timbering. The timber-framed Bridge Cottage stands by the church. The centre of the old village is marked by a cross, said to have been erected by the de Beauchamp family in the fifteenth century. The cross at its top was destroyed by Puritans and later replaced with an eighteenth-century urn from the churchyard. The Old Manor House, nearby, dates from the fourteenth century and is built of Cotswold stone. The Cross House, opposite, is dated 1711. Childswickham House, formerly called the William and Mary House, is dated 1698 and in the 1870s was thought to be haunted by the ghost of the 'Blue Lady'. The parish church of St Mary the Virgin has a slender fifteenth-century stone spire, which can be seen for miles around.

Cropthorne Mill
Fladbury

According to Haviland's *History of Fladbury* (1872), 'while the ground on which the town of Evesham stands was a wilderness, Fladbury was a place of such importance as to contain a monastery and to be worth giving by a king to a bishop.' The king was Ethelred of Mercia, the bishop Oftfor of Worcester and the year 691. Nothing now remains of this Saxon foundation. Two mills (now private houses) stand on opposite banks of the River Avon: Fladbury Mill, dating from the sixteenth century, is on the western side of the weir, while on the eastern side is Cropthorne Mill, built in about 1700. A small cable ferry operates between the two river banks. On the Cropthorne side, beyond the island on which the mill stands, is Fladbury Lock. A plaque notes that Charles I granted William Sandys of Fladbury the right to make the river navigable on 9 March 1635. In 1795 Ireland observed: 'The country about Fladbury is remarkable for its fertility; a quality which the women in the neighbourhood are said to possess in a degree and at a period of life scarce elsewhere known, it being no uncommon circumstance, as I am informed, for women to bear children when advanced to near the age of fifty.'

Abbey Precincts
Evesham

Situated within a few yards of each other, in what was once the abbey precincts, are the two medieval churches of St Lawrence and All Saints. Both were originally chapelries attached to Evesham Abbey. It is thought that St Lawrence was built exclusively for pilgrims, to allow the townsfolk to worship in All Saints without the risk of catching any contagious diseases. St Lawrence (in the foreground of the photograph) is now in the care of the Redundant Churches Fund. The Bell Tower, built by Abbot Clement Lichfield just before the Dissolution, is one of the few monastic remains. Abbot Reginald's Gateway, situated at the southern end of Market Place, was one of the entrances to the abbey precincts. Built in the twelfth century, the timber-framed buildings above and adjacent to it are probably fifteenth century. The Almonry, dating from the fourteenth or fifteenth century, stands on or near the site of the old monastic almonry. It is now a museum and tourist information centre. Inside is the de Montfort Room, opened in 1965 to commemorate the 700th anniversary of the battle of Evesham.

Priory and Court
Little Malvern

Sheltering beneath the wooded slopes of the Malvern Hills 3 miles south of Great Malvern are the remains of a small Benedictine priory, thought to have been founded in 1125. Tradition, however, holds that it was founded in 1171 by two brothers, Jocelin and Edred of Worcester. The priory was dissolved in about 1537, and all that remains of the priory church is the chancel and central tower. The fourteenth-century Prior's Hall or Refectory has been incorporated into Little Malvern Court, nearby. This 'antique wood-framed building' (Laird) belongs to the Berington family, descendants of John Russell who leased the property after the Dissolution. The village is one of the so called 'Seven Sisters', the others being Malvern Wells, The Wyche (or South Malvern), West Malvern, North Malvern, Malvern Link and Great Malvern. Sir Edward Elgar, the popular English composer, was born in 1857 at Lower Broadheath, 3 miles north-west of Worcester. The cottage is now a museum, containing a unique collection of Elgar memorabilia. Dying on 23 February 1934, Elgar was buried in the cemetery of the Roman Catholic church of St Wulstan, Little Malvern.

Malvern Priory
Great Malvern

Great Malvern Priory, standing on the eastern slopes of the Malvern Hills, was founded in 1085 by Aldwyn, a hermit, with the encouragement of St Wulfstan, the last Saxon Bishop of Worcester. Dedicated to St Mary and St Michael, the house was built on land belonging to Westminster Abbey and, consequently, was always subject to its jurisdiction. The long struggle for supremacy between Worcester and Westminster is exemplified in the quarrel of 1282, which involved not only the abbots and archbishop, but also the king and finally the pope. At the Dissolution the monastic estates and buildings became the property of the Crown and were sold or leased to numerous individuals. The abbey church was bought by the villagers, led by a Malvern man, John Pope, for the sum of £20. It was all the money the 150 families could afford and it left them with no funds to repair the damaged building. The church remained in a bad state of repair until 1860, when it was thoroughly restored by George Gilbert Scott. The north porch was rebuilt in 1894. Inside, referring to six old bell clappers, are the words:

Our duty done in belfry high
Now voiceless tongues at rest we
lie.

Marina and Town
Upton upon Severn

Randall described the former market town of Upton upon Severn in 1862: 'From its position upon the Severn, and its being in the centre of a fruit-producing country, it is the great depot for cider, which is brought down to its wharf, and shipped to all parts of England.' Once a busy and prosperous inland port, carrying produce to and from the port of Bristol, Upton is now a small country town, with a marina servicing the needs of pleasure-boats and river-cruisers. Many of the houses, shops and inns date from the town's heyday: the timber-framed Ye Olde Anchor Inn is dated 1601, while the stuccoed three-storeyed White Lion Hotel and the two-storeyed Talbot Head Hotel are Georgian. All that remains of the old church, damaged in a skirmish towards the end of the Civil War, is the red sandstone bell tower (or The Pepperpot) of about 1300. The 75-foot-high stone section is surmounted by a copper-covered cupola, built in 1769–70 by Anthony Keck. The parish church of St Peter and St Paul at the west end of the town was built by Arthur Blomfield in 1878–9. Dr John Dee, mathematician and astrologer to Elizabeth I, was rector at Upton from 1553 to 1608.

St James's Church
Defford

Defford, its name derived from 'deep ford', lies on a ridge north of the Avon, just off the main road from Pershore to Upton-upon-Severn and the Malverns. The village contains a large number of modern houses with a few black-and-white timber-framed cottages, situated mainly near St James's Church. The upper part of the low square tower of the church is of architectural interest because of its black-and-white timber-framing. One mile north of Defford, at Besford, is the only timber-framed church in Worcestershire. Remarkably, although it was restored in 1881, when the restoration movement was at its peak, the original structure survived. The chancel – a nineteenth-century addition – is, however, built of stone. Even more remarkably, the small church somehow managed to retain its sixteenth-century rood-loft, when nearly all of them were destroyed during the iconoclastic years of Edward VI. Two miles south of Defford, perched high on a ridge above the Avon, is the church of St John the Baptist, Strensham. Inside is a simple wall tablet in memory of Samuel Butler, author of *Hudibras*, who was born at Strensham in 1613.

Toy Cottage
Church Lench

Church Lench, to the north of Evesham and close to the Warwickshire border, is one of a number of black-and-white villages collectively known as The Lenches: Rous Lench, Atch Lench, Ab Lench and Sheriffs Lench being the others. At the time of the Domesday survey of 1086 the land was held by several bishops, including those of Evesham and Worcester. Church Lench is the largest of the group, some 345 feet above sea-level, with views over the Vale of Evesham. The church of All Saints dates from Norman times, with fourteenth- and fifteenth-century alterations and additions. It was much restored in 1850–88. Lench Court at Rous Lench, described as 'one of the most perfect examples of early Tudor architecture in Worcestershire' (Fraser), belonged to the Rous family from 1397 to 1721. Between 1876 and 1916 it was owned by the Rev. W. K. W. Chafy, who was responsible for building the Victorian pillar-box by the village green – set in a miniature gabled house, built of stone and timber. A similar house, bearing the Chafy coat-of-arms, can be found at nearby Radford. There are numerous monuments to the Rous family in the church of St Peter.

The Guildhall
Worcester

In the 1227 charter, granted to Worcester by Henry III, the city was permitted to establish a guild of merchants to control trade within its precincts. The hall in which the medieval guild met quickly became the city's judicial and administrative centre. In 1797 Green referred to the building, which was replaced by the present Guildhall, as the 'old town-hall' and described it as 'a large structure of timber, of longer extent than the present; it had a piazza in front, adjoining to which, next to Cooken-street, was a range of shops facing the High-street.' The old hall contained the courts of justice and the prison, including the notorious dungeon known as 'the peephole'. Work began on rebuilding the Guildhall in 1721 under the direction of Thomas White, a local architect. Built of brick with dressings of stone, it was completed in 1723. North and south wings were added in 1725 and 1727 respectively. The statue of Queen Anne above the main entrance was carved by White, as may have been those of Charles I and Charles II. Restored in 1877–80, the Guildhall still serves as the city's town hall, but the Sessions and Magistrates Courts are held elsewhere.

The Greyfriars
Worcester

In Friar Street, north-east of the Cathedral, is the Greyfriars, originally built in 1480 as a guest-house or hostelry for travellers. It belonged to the adjacent Franciscan friary, of which nothing else remains. Considered by Pevsner to be 'one of the finest timber-framed buildings in the county', the Greyfriars has a 69-foot-long street facade with a large double doorway leading through a cobbled passage to an inner courtyard. With early seventeenth- and late eighteenth-century additions, the house was given to the National Trust in 1966. The Commandery, beside the Worcester and Birmingham Canal in Sidbury, was originally the Hospital of St Wulstan, founded in 1085. The present building, with its Great Hall and medieval wall paintings, dates from the late fifteenth century. In 1545 it became the country home of Thomas Wylde, a wealthy clothier, and remained in the family's possession until 1764. Charles II used the building as his headquarters in 1651 during the battle of Worcester. Today it houses the Civil War Centre, depicting not only the events leading up to the decisive battle but also social and domestic aspects of the period.

St Nicholas's Church
Dormston

The tiny village of Dormston, 6 miles west of Alcester, boasts a fourteenth-century church with a timber-framed west tower, added in about 1450. Dedicated to St Nicholas, it was originally a 'forest church' and on one of the walls of the nave are faint traces of medieval paintings. Built into the south wall, near the altar, is part of the old churchyard cross. Staple holes (now broken) on the octagonal font enabled it to be locked to prevent 'witches' from stealing or polluting the holy water. Dormston Manor, formerly Bag End Farm, dates from about 1600 and has two dovecotes. The timber-framed dovecote at Moat Farm was restored by the Avoncroft Museum of Buildings between 1972 and 1974. It contains over 720 timber nesting-boxes supported on stone piers. The dovecote is of the same period as the gabled, timber-framed Moat Farm, dated 1663. A mile or so east of Dormston is the large village of Inkberrow, with an assortment of houses surrounding the village green. On 10 May 1645, on his way to Naseby, Charles I stayed the night at the old vicarage (rebuilt in 1762) and left behind a book of maps, now carefully preserved.

The Old Rectory
Abbots Morton

At the eastern edge of the county, close to the Warwickshire border, the village of Abbots Morton – running along a single street – contains an outstanding variety of black-and-white houses and cottages, typical of rural Worcestershire. In the centre of the village are two working farms. At the eastern end, houses like 'Cymbeline' and 'Edwalyn Cottage' are built end-on to the street and would once have belonged to the poorer villagers. Those who were better off or more important lived in houses like 'The Old Rectory' and 'Manor Cottage', sited at the western end below the hill-top church of St Peter. 'Corner Thatch', a converted eighteenth-century barn, incorporates a postbox, roofed with thatch. Dating from Norman times, the church stands on the site of a Saxon foundation. It is essentially fourteenth century, with windows of various periods. In the east window of the chancel are Flemish medallions, one dated 1590. The water-filled ditch in the field north-east of the church marks the site of a moated house owned by the abbots of Evesham. Their connection with the village is echoed in its name.

Chantry Cottage
Droitwich

Droitwich is an ancient settlement dating back to at least Roman times. Its Latin name was Salinae, meaning 'salt-works' for which the town became internationally famous. References to its saline springs, said to be ten times saltier than the sea, also occur in the Domesday Book. In about 1540 Leland noted the wholesale destruction of the forests around 'Wiche' to provide fuel for the salt furnaces. He also noted that wood had become so scarce that it had to be sought as far away as Worcester, Bromsgrove, Alvechurch and Alcester. Situated on the River Salwarpe, the small town underwent considerable expansion in the early part of the nineteenth century as a spa. This development was almost entirely due to John Corbett, the 'Salt King', who built the Salters' Hall (1881), the St Andrew's Brine Baths (c. 1887) and converted the sixteenth-century St Andrew's House into the Raven Hotel. The Corbett style, according to Pevsner, is 'brick with half-timbered upper parts'. The Old Cock Inn in Friar Street, licensed in 1712, incorporates two stone heads and a medieval window from the old demolished church of St Nicholas. Chantry Cottage, adjacent, was restored in 1976–7.

12 High Street
Feckenham

Three types of building material can be found in the architecture of Worcestershire: in the south, around Broadway, the properties are of Cotswold stone; around Evesham and the Avon valley the houses are essentially black-and-white; while in the north at Feckenham the buildings are overwhelmingly red brick with timber frames. Nevertheless, Feckenham does contain a mixture of building styles, including black-and-white and Georgian. Five miles south-west of Redditch on an old Roman road (also the Salt Way), the village once stood in the heart of the royal hunting forest of Feckenham, which covered an area of almost 200 square miles and embraced over sixty villages and hamlets. This great medieval woodland has now disappeared, demolished to fuel the salt industry of Droitwich. The parish church of St John the Baptist dates from Norman times but was rebuilt in 1853. The glass in the east window of the aisle depicts John de Feckenham (or John Howman), the son of a local woodcutter, who became the last Abbot of Westminster, dying in 1585. Hanbury Hall, a red-brick house of 1701 and owned by the National Trust, is 4 miles to the west.

The Stable and Barn
Avoncroft Museum

Dating from the fourteenth to the mid-twentieth century, the buildings at Avoncroft have all been saved from destruction. The first property to be rescued, repaired and re-erected on the open-air site was the fifteenth-century timber-framed Merchant's House from Bromsgrove. It originally stood on the corner of Station Street and Worcester Road. Since 1967, when the museum first opened, over twenty buildings have been preserved. The Stable, with its brick-infilled elm-timber frame, dates from the late eighteenth century and was used to shelter working horses at Ridgeway Court Farm, Wychbold. The Barn, built using a cruck-frame probably in the sixteenth century, came from Cholstrey Court Farm near Leominster. The spaces between the wall timbers are woven with split oak pales, supported by staves. Avoncroft Museum of Buildings, opened in 1967, is at Stoke Heath, 2 miles south of Bromsgrove. Its main purpose, however, is not to collect buildings but to prevent their destruction. Indeed, the policy, wherever possible, is to preserve buildings on their original site, and move them only as a last resort.

St Michael's Church
Rochford

Standing on the low-lying southern bank of the River Teme, just over 2 miles east of Tenbury Wells, is the church of St Michael, Rochford. Essentially twelfth-century, with a timber bell-turret and spire, the church has a weathered Norman tympanum, decorated with the Tree of Life, over the blocked north doorway. The east window contains some very early glass by William Morris (c. 1863) which Pevsner rates as being 'infinitely superior to anything done at the time in England or abroad'. The name of the village is derived from 'rock ford', after a convenient crossing-point of the river formed by flat slabs of sandstone rock. In most villages the church stands on high ground above the homes of its parishioners. At Rochford the reverse is true, with the houses and farms sited on rising ground above the church. On the opposite side of the river is Knighton-on-Teme, once the site of a medieval village, probably abandoned after the plague of 1348–9. The only building to survive is the Norman church of St Michael, with a shingled bell-turret of 1959. Traces of the deserted settlement can still be found in the surrounding fields.

The Orangery
Witley Court

Once one of the most palatial country houses in England, Witley Court is now a spectacular ruin. The first mansion was built in the late seventeenth century by Thomas Foley, son of a Stourbridge ironmaster, on the site of a large Jacobean house, about 200 yards away from the medieval parish church of Great Witney (now demolished). His grandson, also Thomas (later Baron Foley of Kidderminster), carried out extensive enlargements to the mansion. In the process of extending the existing park the old village and rectory were demolished. Further additions and alterations continued over the years – including John Nash's Ionic porticoes, built in about 1800 – and culminating in the Italianate-style rebuilding of about 1860 by Samuel Daukes for the 1st Earl of Dudley. After the disastrous fire of 1937, the house fell into ruin and decay. In the gardens are the remains of a 26-foot-high sculpted fountain. The present parish church, considered to be the finest baroque church in Britain, was built in 1733–5 on a new site closer to the mansion. It is noted for the richness of its interior decoration, among which are ceiling paintings by Antonio Bellucci.

Teme Valley
near Stanford on Teme

Scattered along the Teme Valley eastward from Tenbury Wells are exceptionally high hedges, some up to 10 feet tall, grown to shelter hopyards from the wind. The hop plant (*Humulus lupulus*) is trained to grow on a network of twine along a forest of specially erected poles. In the past the vertical string up which the long stem of the plant entwines itself was tied to the top wire frame by farm-workers balanced on long stilts. Today most of the work is done by machine. Duncumb wrote in 1804: 'Hop plantations prevail in different degrees throughout the county; but are most frequent towards Worcestershire. They were, probably, made here soon after the introduction of hops into England, which was about the year 1524.' In fact, hops were first introduced into England in about 1400 through the Kent ports. Large-scale cultivation began in the sixteenth century, with Hampshire, Herefordshire, Worcestershire and later Kent becoming the most important hop-growing areas. Although male and female plants are cultivated, only the fruit cones of the female are used to clarify, preserve and flavour beer.

PHOTOGRAPHER'S NOTES

Living in the centre of the Heart of England, I seemed to be ideally situated for a project like this. Everywhere was near to home, and naturally I was already familiar with all the very best places. It seemed idyllic. Quite simply, all I needed to do was pop out when the weather was suitable, take a snap or two and pop home again for a cup of tea. Well, I can dream.

As I started this book it occurred to me that I probably knew places like Yorkshire and the Lake District more intimately, a fact that would certainly have to change. I had produced books within my own home counties: following the journey of the River Avon from source to Severn and exploring Shropshire from the point of view of a twelfth-century monk, Brother Cadfael. Both of these obviously restricted what I could see or take pictures of. The Heart of England, however, presented me with a marvellous opportunity to explore, in a broader sense, many of the attractions of this beautiful area, and see it afresh through the eyes of a visitor.

Maps, books, brochures and leaflets were studied and a massive list produced of places to visit. This gave me a valuable insight into the diversity of subject matter within the Heart of England. Each place was visited to check the best time of day for photography and to anticipate how the scene would look in England's varying weathers. Compass readings were taken, notes made, and occasionally, if lucky, a shot taken straight away. More often than not, however, another visit was required. Many fine opportunities for photography were missed as I attempted to take pictures without people or cars, and so create something of a timeless scene. Many more opportunities were missed as I scurried around picking up litter, so carelessly dropped and so unsightly in any photograph. But, eventually, the pictures were taken, each adding to a growing body of work.

As the number of shots increase, so editing becomes more difficult. The Country Series is designed to accommodate no more than about 130 photographs. A delicate balance, therefore, needs to be maintained if an area is to be properly represented. Being able to work so closely on such tasks with the writer, Robin Whiteman, is extremely useful. Each picture is studied from different professional viewpoints, resulting hopefully in the selection of pictures that sit nicely together, giving an accurate flavour of an area and offering the reader a valuable and informative insight into the delights available.

The camera used was a 35mm Nikon F3, a tool I have owned for many years and which now has a rather lovely battered appearance. It remains totally reliable. Lenses ranged from 24mm wide-angle to 180 telephoto, all Nikkor. Film was Fuji Velvia, tripod – medium-sized Gitzo, filters – a polarizer, the warming 81 series and a graduated neutral-density.

Rob Talbot

SELECTED PROPERTIES

ENGLISH HERITAGE

All English Heritage properties, except where specified, are open from April to end September every day from 10am to 6pm and from October to March, Tuesdays to Sundays, from 10am to 4pm, and are closed on 24, 25 and 26 December and 1 January.

Head Office
Keysign House, 429 Oxford Street, London W1R 2HD
Tel: (071) 973 3000

Midland Regional Information Office
Finchfield House, Castlecroft Road, Wolverhampton WV3 8BY
Tel: (0902) 765105
Fax: 0902 766245

Boscobel House
Brewood, Shropshire ST19 9AR
Tel: (0902) 850244

Buildwas Abbey
Ironbridge, Telford, Shropshire TF8 7BW
Tel: (0952) 433274

Goodrich Castle
Goodrich, Ross-on-Wye, Hereford & Worcester HR9 6HY
Tel: (0600) 890538

Haughmond Abbey
Upton Magna, Uffington, Shrewsbury, Shropshire SY4 4RW
Tel: (0743) 77661

Kenilworth Castle
Kenilworth, Warwickshire
Tel: (0926) 52078
Open: daily throughout the year except 25 December and 1 January

Lilleshall Abbey
Abbey Road, Lilleshall, Shropshire TF10 9HW
Tel: (0952) 604431
Open: daily throughout the year

Mortimer's Cross Water Mill
The Mill House, Mortimer's Cross, nr Leominster, Hereford & Worcester HR6 9PE
Tel: (0568) 818820
Open: April to end September, Thursdays and Sundays only and Bank Holidays

Stokesay Castle
Craven Arms, Shropshire SY7 9AH
Tel: (0588) 672544
Open: March to end October, except Tuesdays; November, weekends only

Wall Roman Site (Letocetum)
Wall, nr Lichfield, Staffordshire WS14 0AW
Tel: (0543) 480768

Wenlock Priory
Much Wenlock, Shropshire TF13 0HS
Tel: (0952) 727466

Witley Court
Great Witley, Hereford & Worcester
Tel: (0299) 896341

Wroxeter Roman City
Wroxeter, Shropshire SY5 6PH
Tel: (0743) 761330

NATIONAL TRUST

Mercia Region
Regional Public Affairs Department, Attingham Park, Shrewsbury SY4 4TP
Tel: (0743) 77343

Severn Region
Regional Public Affairs Department, Mythe End House, Tewkesbury GL20 6EB
Tel: (0684) 850051

Attingham Park
Shrewsbury, Shropshire SY4 4TP
Tel: (0743) 77203
Open: March to end September, Saturdays to Wednesdays; October, Saturdays and Sundays; Bank Holiday Mondays Deer Park and Grounds Open: daily throughout the year, except 25 December

Baddesley Clinton
Knowle, Solihull B93 0DQ
Tel: (0564) 783294
Open: March to end October, Wednesdays to Sundays; Bank Holiday Mondays Closed Good Friday

Benthall Hall
Broseley, Shropshire TF12 5RX
Tel: (0952) 882159
Open: March to end September, Wednesdays, Sundays and Bank Holiday Mondays

Berrington Hall
nr Leominster, Hereford & Worcester HR6 0DW
Tel: (0568) 615721
Open: Easter to end April, Saturdays and Sundays; May to end September, Wednesdays to Sundays; October, Saturdays and Sundays; Bank Holiday Mondays

Biddulph Grange Garden
Biddulph Grange, Biddulph, Stoke-on-Trent, Staffordshire ST8 7SD
Tel: (0782) 517999
Open: May to end October, Wednesdays to Sundays; November to December, Saturdays and Sundays; Bank Holiday Mondays

Charlecote Park
Wellesbourne, Warwickshire CV35 9ER
Tel: (0789) 470277
Open: March to end October, daily except Mondays and Thursdays; Bank Holiday Mondays

Coughton Court
nr Alcester, Warwickshire B49 5JA
Tel: (0789) 762435
Open: Easter to April, Saturdays and Sundays; May to end September, daily except Mondays and Fridays; Bank Holiday Mondays

Croft Castle
nr Leominster, Hereford & Worcester HR6 9PW
Tel: (0568) 85246
Open: Easter to April and October, Saturdays and Sundays; May to end September, Wednesdays to Sundays; Bank Holiday Mondays

Dudmaston
Quatt, nr Bridgnorth, Shropshire WV15
6QN
Tel: (0746) 780866
*Open: April to end September,
Wednesdays and Sundays only*

Farnborough Hall
Banbury, Oxfordshire OX17 1DU
*Open: April to end September,
Wednesdays and Saturdays; Terraced
Walk only, Thursdays and Fridays*

The Greyfriars
Friar Street, Worcester WR1 2LZ
Tel: (0905) 23571
*Open: April to end October, Wednesdays,
Thursdays and Bank Holiday Mondays*

Hanbury Hall
Droitwich, Hereford & Worcester WR9
7EA
Tel: (0527) 84214
*Open: April to end of October, Saturdays,
Sundays and Mondays*

Lower Brockhampton
Bringsty, Hereford & Worcester WR6
5UH
Tel: (0885) 483075
*Open: Easter to end October, Wednesdays
to Sundays, and Bank Holiday Mondays*

Moseley Old Hall
Fordhouses, Wolverhampton WV10 7HY
Tel: (0902) 782808
*Open: mid March to end October,
Wednesdays, Saturdays, Sundays and
Bank Holiday Mondays; July and August,
also Tuesdays*

Packwood House
Lapworth, Solihull B94 6AT
Tel: (0564) 782024
*Open: Easter to October, Wednesdays to
Sundays, and Bank Holiday Mondays*

Shugborough Estate
Milford, nr Stafford, Staffordshire ST17
0XB
Tel: (0889) 881388
Open: daily mid March to October

Upton House
Banbury, Oxfordshire OX15 6HT
Tel: (0295) 87266
*Open: Easter to end April and October,
Saturdays and Sundays; May to end
September, Saturdays to Wednesdays;
Bank Holiday Mondays*

Westbury Court Garden
Westbury-on-Severn, Gloucestershire
GL14 1PD
Tel: (0452) 76461
*Open: Easter to end October, Wednesdays
to Sundays, and Bank Holiday Mondays*

Wightwick Manor
Wightwick Bank, Wolverhampton WV6
8EE
Tel: (0902) 761108
*Open: March to end December,
Thursdays and Saturdays; Bank Holiday
Sundays and Mondays*

Wilderhope Manor
Easthope, Much Wenlock, Shropshire
TF13 6EG
Tel: (069 43) 363
*Open: April to end September,
Wednesdays and Saturdays; October to
end March, Saturdays only*

SHAKESPEARE BIRTHPLACE TRUST

All properties are open daily throughout
the year except 24, 25 and 26 December.

Anne Hathaway's Cottage
Shottery, Stratford-upon-Avon,
Warwickshire CV37 9HH
Tel: (0789) 292100

Shakespeare's Birthplace
Henley Street, Stratford-upon-Avon,
Warwickshire CV37 6QW
Tel: (0789) 204016

Hall's Croft
Old Town, Stratford-upon-Avon,
Warwickshire CV37 6BG
Tel: (0789) 292107

**Mary Arden's House and Countryside
Museum**
Wilmcote, Stratford-upon-Avon,
Warwickshire CV37 9UN
Tel: (0789) 293455

New Place and Nash's House
Chapel Street, Stratford-upon-Avon,
Warwickshire CV37 6EP
Tel: (0789) 292325

MISCELLANEOUS

The Heart of England Tourist Board
Woodside, Larkhill Road, Worcester
WR5 2EF
Tel: (0905) 763436

Arbury Hall
Nuneaton, Warwickshire
Tel: (0203) 382804
*Open: Easter to September, Sundays and
Bank Holiday Mondays; July and August,
also Tuesdays and Wednesdays*

Avoncroft Museum of Buildings
Stoke Heath, Bromsgrove, Hereford &
Worcester B60 4JR
Tel: (0527) 31886/31363
*Open: March and November, Tuesday to
Thursday, Saturdays and Sundays; April
to October, Tuesdays to Sundays; Bank
Holidays*

Black Country Museum
Tipton Road, Dudley DY1 4SQ
Tel: (021) 577 9643
*Open: daily throughout the year except 25
December*

Coombe Abbey Country Park
Brinklow Road, Binley, nr Coventry CV3
2AB
Tel: Ranger's Office (0203) 453720
Open: daily throughout the year

Dinmore Manor
near Hereford HR4 8EE
Tel: (0432) 830322
Open: daily throughout the year

Dudley Zoo and Castle
2 The Broadway, Dudley DY1 4QB
Tel: (0384) 252401
*Open: daily throughout the year except 25
December*

Ironbridge Gorge Museum
(Visitor Information Service), Ironbridge,
Telford, Shropshire TF8 7AW
Tel: (0952) 433522 or (0952) 432751/
432166 (weekends)
*Open: daily throughout the year except 24
and 25 December; some small sites closed
from November to February*

Lord Leycester's Hospital
Warwick, Warwickshire CV34 4BH
Tel: (0926) 491422/492797
*Open: daily throughout the year except
Sundays, Good Friday and 25 December*

Ludlow Castle
Castle Square, Ludlow, Shropshire
Tel: (0584) 873947
Open: daily from February to December

Ragley Hall
Alcester, Warwickshire B49 5NJ
Tel: (0789) 762090
*Open: House and Park, April to end
September; House only, Tuesday to
Thursday, Saturdays and Sundays, and
Bank Holiday Mondays; Park and
Adventure Wood, every day in July and
August*

**Royal Shakespeare Theatre, Swan
Theatre, and The Other Place**
Stratford-upon-Avon
For all bookings telephone: (0789)
295623
24 hour booking information: (0789)
269191

Selly Manor Museum
c/o Bournville Village Trust, Estate Office,
Oak Tree Lane, Bournville B30 1UB
Tel: (021) 4720199
Manor location: corner of Maple Road
and Sycamore Road, Bournville
*Open: mid-January to mid-December,
Tuesdays to Fridays and Bank Holidays
from Easter to end August*

Tamworth Castle and Museum
Holloway, Tamworth, Staffordshire B79
7LR
Tel: (0827) 63563
Open: daily throughout the year

Warwick Castle
Warwick, Warwickshire CV34 4QU
Tel: (0926) 495421
Open: every day except Christmas Day

SELECT BIBLIOGRAPHY

Anderson, John Corbet, *Shropshire: Its Early History and Antiquities*, Willis and Sotheran, London, 1864

Bilbey, David, *Church Stretton*, Phillimore, Chichester, 1985

Bird, John, *Stratford-upon-Avon Official Guide*, Stratford District Council, 1979

Blackwall, Anthony, *Historic Bridges of Shrewsbury*, Shropshire Libraries, Shrewsbury, 1985

Boston, Noel, *The Story of Lilleshall Abbey*, Newport Advertiser, 1934

Bottomly, Frank, *The Explorer's Guide to the Abbeys, Monasteries and Churches of Great Britain*, Avenel Books, New York, 1981

Brewer, J. Norris, *The Beauties of England and Wales: Warwickshire* (vol 15), Harris, London, 1814

Camden, William, *Britannia*, Edmund Gibson, London, 1695

Defoe, Daniel, *A Tour through the Whole Island of Great Britain*, 1724–6 (republished: Penguin, Harmondsworth, 1971)

Dugdale, Sir William, *The Antiquities of Warwickshire*, (revised and augmented by Dr W. Thomas), London, 1730

Duncumb, John, *Collections towards the History and Antiquities of Hereford* (vol 1), Wright, Hereford, 1804

Eyton, Rev. R. W., *Antiquities of Shropshire* (12 vols), John Russell Smith, London, 1854–60

Field, William, *An Historical and Descriptive Account of the Town and Castle of Warwick and the Neighbouring Spa of Leamington*, Sharpe, 1815

Fox, Levi, *Historic Stratford-upon-Avon*, Jarrold, Norwich, 1986

Fox, Levi, *The Shakespearian Properties*, Jarrold, Norwich, 1981

Fraser, Maxwell, *Companion into Worcestershire*, Methuen, London, 1939

Garner, Lawrence, *Shropshire* (Shire County Guide: 7), Shire, Aylesbury, 1985

Green, Valentine, *The History & Antiquities of the City and Suburbs of Worcester* (vols 1–2), Green, London, 1796

Hannett, John, *The Forest of Arden, its Towns, Villages and Hamlets*, Simpkin, Marshall, & Co., 1863

Havins, Peter J. Neville, *Portrait of Worcestershire*, Hale, London, 1974

Hawthorne, Nathaniel, *Our Home Town*, Walter Scott, London, 1863

Ireland, Samuel, *Picturesque Views on the Upper, or Warwickshire Avon*, Faulder, 1795

Jackson, Michael, *Castles of Shropshire*, Shropshire Libraries, Shrewsbury, 1988

Jennett, Sean, ed., *The Shakespeare Country and South Warwickshire*, Darton, Longman & Todd, 1965

Kissack, Keith, *The River Wye*, Dalton, Lavenham, 1978

Laird, F. C., *A Topographical and Historical Description of the County of Worcester*, London, 1814

Leland, John, *The Itinerary* (5 vols), ed. Lucy Toul'min Smith, Southern Illinois University Press, Carbondale, 1964

Lloyd, Revd R. H., *Bredon Hill and its Villages* (local guide), 1967

Midmer, Roy, *English Medieval Monasteries 1066–1540*, Heinemann, London, 1979

Nash, J., *History and Antiquities of Worcestershire*, London, 1781–2

Owen, H. and Blakeway, J. B., *A History of Shrewsbury* (2 vols), Harding, Lepard and Co., 1825

Peachey, Stuart, *The Edge Hill Campaign & the Letters of Nehemiah Wharton*, Partizan, Leigh-on-Sea, 1989

Pevsner, Nikolaus, *Herefordshire* (The Buildings of England series), Penguin Books, Harmondsworth, 1963

Pevsner, Nikolaus, *Shropshire* (The Buildings of England series), Penguin Books, Harmondsworth, 1958

Pevsner, Nikolaus, *Staffordshire* (The Buildings of England series), Penguin Books, Harmondsworth, 1974

Pevsner, Nikolaus, *Warwickshire* (The Buildings of England series), Penguin Books, Harmondsworth, 1966

Pevsner, Nikolaus, *Worcestershire* (The Buildings of England series), Penguin Books, Harmondsworth, 1968

Pringle, Roger, ed., *Poems of Warwickshire: An Anthology*, Roundwood, Kineton, 1980

Randall, J., *The Severn Valley*, James S. Virtue, London, 1862

Raven, Michael, *A Shropshire Gazetteer*, Raven, Market Drayton, 1989

Richardson, Kenneth, *Coventry: Past into Present*, Phillimore, Chichester, 1987

Robinson, Rev. Charles J., *A History of the Mansions and Manors of Herefordshire*, Longmans, London, 1872

Rudder, Samuel, *A New History of Gloucestershire*, Rudder, Cirencester, 1779

Thorn, Frank and Caroline, eds., *Domesday Book: Shropshire*, Phillimore, Chichester, 1986

Thorne, James, *Rambles by Rivers: The Avon*, Knight, 1845

Thorold, Henry, *A Shell Guide: Staffordshire*, Faber & Faber, London, 1978

Timmins, Sam, *A History of Warwickshire*, Stock, 1889

Tonkin, J. W., *Herefordshire*, Batsford, 1977

Trinder, Barrie, *A History of Shropshire*, Phillimore, Chichester, 1983

Victoria History of the County of Warwick, Oxford University Press

Victoria History of the County of Worcester, St Catherine's Press, 1924

Waite, Vincent, *Malvern Country*, Dent, London, 1968

Waite, Vincent, *Shropshire Hill Country*, Dent, London, 1970

Warwick, Frances, Countess of, *Warwick Castle and its Earls*, Hutchinson, 1903

Wright, Thomas, *The History of Ludlow and its Neighbourhood*, Jones, Ludlow, 1852

Young, Peter, *Edgehill 1642*, Roundwood, Kineton, 1976

INDEX

Page numbers in *italics* denote photographs.